A DRIVER'S MANUAL
*CAR®
FOR DRUNK DRIVERS

*Cognitive Apprenticeship Recovery

Maurice "Mo" Murray

authorHOUSE®

AuthorHouse™ LLC
1663 Liberty Drive
Bloomington, IN 47403
www.authorhouse.com
Phone: 1-800-839-8640

Published by AuthorHouse 11/11/2013

ISBN: 978-1-4918-0838-2 (sc)
ISBN: 978-1-4918-0837-5 (e)

Library of Congress Control Number: 2013914715

Dedicated to…

The alcoholic who is still out there suffering…

Let's work on this together.

The Greatest Discovery…

"The greatest discovery of the 19th century was not the realm of physical sciences, but the power of the subconscious mind touched by faith. Any individual can tap into an eternal reservoir of power that will enable them to overcome any problem that may arise. All weaknesses can be overcome…"

William James
Harvard Psychologist
The Father of American Psychology

Table of Contents

Foreword

Years ago, when my daughter was about 9 years old, she went to her mother for some help on a homework problem. The reply came: "Ask your father; he's a wealth of unrelated information."

I have also been compared to the man in Stephen Leacock's "Nonsense Novels" who jumps on his horse and charges off in all four directions at the same time.

So, help with your recovery does come with a price tag. You'll have to suffer through several of my corny stories, many of which, you'll soon see, are related to "aviation." My father was an extremely positive influence in my life. He built the first airplane that he ever flew (in the 1920's) and finally relinquished his pilot's license voluntarily at the age of 74. He got to see me flying "straight and level" before he died! Also, I use a lot of quotations. I quote:

I know heaps of quotations, so I can always make a fair show of knowledge.

(O. Douglas)

I always have a quotation for everything, it saves original thinking.

(Dorothy L. Sayers)

In a way, the quotations are not random. Here are the categories:

1) **"Smoker,"** i.e., Put that in your pipe and smoke it!

2) **"Grow Up or Throw Up!"** These are sentimental stories or well-worn aphorisms that seem to empower some and cause others to gag.

3) **"Word,"** i.e., "A word to the wise is sufficient."

4) **"Malarkey,"** i.e., The opposite of "Word." Meaningless talk, as in "Irish malarkey."

5) **"If only I had shot him when I first met him!"** Referring to the misery and the sobriety-threatening situations to which men have subjected women.

6) **"Under every skirt there is a slip!"** Referring to the misery and the sobriety-threatening situations to which women have subjected men.

You'll always have the benefit of Finnegan, our little Irish leprechaun, nearby to point out each of these gems.

In summary, the "Recovering Community" has been called (among other things) "The Great Society of Borrowers." I plead guilty! I'm an "eclectic / borrower." I remember well, especially those things that help me in my recovery!

You are told in the rooms of AA and other treatment venues to take what helps and "throw the rest away!" The pages that follow are "The Best Of" what has helped me and what I've noticed has helped most of my newfound, adopted family. Use it or lose it!

Preface

A Driver's Manual for Drunk Drivers" is the third of my "How To" Recovery books. Each book has further enhanced "Cognitive Apprenticeship Recovery" as a treatment methodology. With each book I have become more aware of my role as a compiler rather than an author. In a very real sense these books have been written by "the Recovering Community" for "the Recovering Community."

Chapter 8 was added when a friend and valued reviewer made the comment "Actually Mo, books about Recovery set my teeth on edge!" I realized then, that jokes about drunks aren't funny to the sober public. However, the recognition that sober alcoholics are actually laughing at their past behaviors from the new perspective of recovery, should be encouraging to everyone. Laughter heals!

The inclusion of a few of my old "As Memory Serves Me" radio scripts and newspaper columns from the late 60's and early 70's, came from the insight of my AA family. They felt that my own "drunk-alog" which is woven within the entire text of the book seemed "too clinical." These few childhood glimpses should soften my technocratic image and lend insight into my unorthodox emphasis on spirituality in everyday life. I was, after all, raised in a "haunted house" which is now owned by all the citizens of the State of Delaware. "Woodburn" the beloved "haunted house" of my childhood is now the Governor's Mansion of The State of Delaware. There are "spirits" and then there are "spirits" … spoken like a true alcoholic.

Concise Car®

The rubrics of CAR® are similar to other Cognitive Apprenticeship Methodology's: "Watch It Do It Know It." CAR's unique power to facilitate recovery is derived by adding the ingredients of "The Way of Analogy" and "The Concept of The Singular."

You might want to start by first reading Chapter 5: The chair's fixed, relax and sit in it as a way to preempt any confusion about how "The Way of Analogy" is being used in "Relationship Associations." Here is the traditional (Thomas Aquinas) "Way of Analogy": Red is Red: and yet a horse is Red, with a "horsey" Redness. CAR® melds this with "The Concept of the Singular" [i.e. Remember Philosophy 101. The Universal Chair of the Greeks was the perfect chair; then came "the Particular" chair (Lounge Chairs); then came "the Singular" chair (your Dad's old Morris chair with the cigar burns on the right arm)] to get its synergism. CAR® is a "Singular Analogous Relationship Driven"

Recovery modality and as such, less easily defined than experienced.

CAR® methodology is already at work "within" you even before you start to read these books. You already know (you are ultimately aware) that you are "within the answer."

"The 'Good News' is... you are in Recovery now!" This is proclaimed at the beginning of all three books.

"The first step in the acquisition of wisdom is silence, the second listening, the third memory, the fourth practice, the fifth teaching others."

Solomon Ibn Gabriol

Respectfully submitted... Maurice "Mo" Murray

[Reference: The Practice of Cognitive Apprenticeship Recovery.

Maurice J Murray, Bowers-Stokesbury Press. Wilmington, DE 1993]

Introduction

The "Good News" is ... you are "in recovery" **now!**

This is absolutely true!

Even if you are still drinking or drugging!

Recovery is no longer just a wish or a dream!

You are "in recovery"!

Congratulations and ...

Welcome! If you're like most of us, it's been one **hell** of a struggle!

Now ... Pause for just a moment ... this is very important, so ... really pause ... and realize ... and acknowledge ... that ... **it is you, yourself, and you ... alone** ... who first recognized this! My words are not an insight but an affirmation!

Saint Augustine said that religion is "faith seeking understanding." In an identical way, without being able to give a sufficient reason, you know that you are "in recovery." You have faith! Now all you need is some help with a few crucial questions ... "What's going on?" "How do I get to where I need to be?" "How do I keep from relapsing?" and "What recovery 'tips' help most?"

Let's start with a multiple-choice question: How are Faith and Sobriety alike?

1) Neither one can drive a school bus.
2) Faith is not a "will to believe."
3) Sobriety is not a "will to stop drinking."
4) Both Faith and Sobriety are encounters with a new love relationship.
5) Faith is Freedom!
6) Sobriety is Freedom!
7) All of the above.
8) None of the above.

If your answer is #7: This Driver's Manual is for you!

If your answer is not #7: This Driver's Manual is for you!

Here's the first of the aviation stories. It was one of my Dad's favorites. He used it whenever I seemed baffled about one of "life's situations." He used it a lot!! Like all of his others, it started with "Son," and then he'd pause, as all great storytellers tend to do, to rivet my attention . . .

"Son . . . The saddest words a pilot has to say when flying in bad weather conditions are **"I can hear you tower . . . but I can't see the runway!"** Then he'd pause again. A very reassuring smile would appear, and he'd continue, "The happiest words a pilot has to say when flying in bad weather conditions are, **"I can hear you tower . . . and I can see the runway!"**

Today, at long last . . . you not only hear the tower . . . you see the runway!

From now on you are in control!

You are, in fact, a lot like Sherlock Holmes. The fascinating thing about this most famous of all detectives was not that he solved the murder, but that right from the beginning, before anyone else, he seemed to understand more of the mystery. That's what we're about in these few short pages. Successful recovery leaves clues . . . so get out your magnifying glass, here we go!

As memory
serves me
By Mo Murray
Friendly recollections of people, places and events
in the not-too-distant past.

Secret Mission Club

My big brother and I used to have a secret mission club. You probably had one too – or something like it. The purpose of our club was to spy on Mr. Thompson, the town atheist. All the kids in the neighborhood were convinced Mr. Thompson would eat people.

As bad luck would have it, our first mission was delayed because of brussel sprouts. Whenever we had brussel sprouts for dinner, the number I was forced to eat had to be carefully negotiated. As I'm sure you may have done in similar circumstances, delaying tactics were a necessary part of the procedure.

Now, by the time the brussel sprouts negotiating was settled, the evening of our first secret mission had turned cool and damp. My brother and I – in appropriate spy fashion – crawled out of the cellar door and through the grape arbor. The fact that we muddied the knees of our knickers in the process didn't bother us. But strange noises from the big back barn did. So we wasted no time scooting down the white cinder-patched alley to the hedgerow behind Mr. Thompson's house.

There he was – chewing away and raking leaves. Actually, according to my brother, Mr. Thompson had already eaten all the people scheduled for that day. So – darnit – I missed the best part . . . all because of my brussel sprout delay.

Still, we watched Mr. Thompson until it got dark. Then we dashed back through our cellar door. I was out of breath. Our first mission had been very exciting – and therefore a great success.

When we first formed our secret mission club, my brother was the chief. He got the top job for three reasons. First, he had all the secret mission passes. Actually, they were tickets left over from the local movie shows. Second, my brother had dibber's rights on all the good meeting places under back porches. And third, my brother was a member of the school safety patrol, so he had a shoulder harness and badge to wear on our secret missions.

Two years later, when my brother retired from his post as chief, I swapped my new stainless steel steam engine for his complete secret mission kit. It was composed of one used safety patrol belt and harness, an old pair of knickers with muddy knees, a tinfoil badge, and a tattered sixth grade reader my brother hadn't turned in. On the front was a picture of a patrol boy. You know, it looked a little like me, when I got everything on.

As memory serves me . . . when my brother retired, I became club president, mission director, and sole owner of all remaining secret mission passes. It didn't seem to bother me at the time that there were no other members.

Say . . . how about joining a nifty secret mission club? All we need is a meeting place under a porch. But, don't worry, you don't need a safety patrol belt and harness. After all, I guess it was a little conspicuous for a spy.

1

The People of the Lie!

Problem drinking (moderate drinking plus one) has nothing to do with Denial. Problem drinking has everything to do with LYING! Denial as it relates to substance abuse is thought of as an "evasive action" taken by the "targeted" abuser. It isn't. It's a lie!

In the rooms of AA "DENIAL" is an acronym for:

"Don't Even Notice I Am Lying!"

That pinpoints the pathology. This Japanese Proverb operationalizes it:

"A man lies to others so that he may lie to himself!"

Having a million ways of lying is not really a good use
of our creativity.

I can't resist illustrating this with a story from The Big Book:

"The alcoholic is like a tornado roaring his way through the lives of others. Hearts are broken. Sweet relationships are dead. Affections have been uprooted. Selfish and inconsiderate habits have kept the home in turmoil. We feel a man is unthinking when he says that sobriety is enough. He is like the farmer who came up out of his

1

cyclone cellar to find his home ruined. To his wife, he remarked, "Don't see anything the matter here, Ma. Ain't it grand the wind stopped blowin?'" [The Big Book page 82]

Elizabeth Loftus clinically explains that a lie is a failure of "source memory."

50 million Americans "struggle" with alcohol but only 10% of them will ever receive treatment!

The fair question: Why do you drink?

The honest answer: I drink because I want to drink! [not because your Mother left you in a burning Circus when you were a kid]

"I'm very functional and lovable when I'm drunk. I'm just like Dudley Moore in the movie 'Authur.'"

Try this "functionality" on for size: Alcohol caused 23,000 automobile deaths last year. The legal term is "Guilty of Vehicular Homicide." And here's where the claim to "functionality" collapses… only 16 % of these fatalities were caused by known chronic repeat drinkers! The other 84% (19,320 deaths) were caused by "functional drinkers."

"…and all the King's Horses and all the King's Men, couldn't put Humpty Dumpty together again!" (English nursery rhyme)

Psychobabble puts it this way: "We want to find the Justification Mythology for Drinking."

AA puts it this way: "We want to find the "Stinkin' Thinkin'"

Mark Twain said "I never write Metropolis when I get paid the same nickel for writing City." So it's a lie and not "Justification Mythology!"

"Sometimes we stumble upon the truth. Fortunately most of us are able to pick ourselves up and proceed as if nothing had happened."

Winston Churchill

I'm not an alcoholic. I'm a social drinker with blackouts.

Drinking is a "learned skill" and I'm a "skilled learner."

The Tragic Story of Audrey Kishline

In 1993 Audrey Kishline founded and became the self appointed president of "Moderation Management." Having experienced her own drinking problems for many years she established a noncoercive program (as opposed to AA's rigid model of: Total Abstinence and Surrender to a "Higher Power.") of common sense support groups for people who wanted to only reduce their drinking and by so doing portray a success story of <u>self control</u>!

The concept of MM came to her almost as an epiphany...

"One afternoon, as I was driving home on the freeway, a question crossed my mind. It went something like this:

There are thousands of support groups available in our country for *chronic* drinkers who have made the decision to abstain from alcohol. Why aren't there any support groups available for *problem* drinkers who have made the decision to moderate their drinking behavior?"

[Kishline, A "Moderate Drinking, The New Option for Problem Drinkers." Tucson, AZ: See Sharp Press, 1994.]

[Note: This very same freeway, (Interstate 90 near Seattle) was to become the scene of the tragic end to this story.]

The book cited above became an immediate best seller. Audrey appeared on all the major TV talk shows: Oprah, Dateline NBC, Good Morning America, ABC World News Tonight and she spoke to large crowds across the country. Here was her proposal...

The "Moderation Management"
Weekly Drinking Guidelines:

Males:
- A maximum of four (4) drinks per day.
- A maximum of fourteen (14) drinks per week.

Females:
- A maximum of three (3) drinks per day.
- A maximum of nine (9) drinks per week.

On the night of March 25, 2000, 911 operators, in Seattle, began answering calls from worried motorists on Washington's Interstate 90 who were reporting that a pickup truck was driving West in the Eastbound lane:

Operator: 911, what are you reporting?

Caller: I would like to report a vehicle going up the wrong way on the freeway near exit 78 about a split second ago.

Operator: Is it a black pickup?

Caller: Yeah, it was black.

Operator: OK, yeah, we have a report of that. Thanks for calling.

Audrey Kishline was the driver of that pickup. She was driving with a blood-alcohol level nearly three times the legal limit. In just minutes the 911 calls changed to report a violent accident.

Operator: 911, what are you reporting?

Caller: I'm reporting a head-on collision on Snoqualmie Pass. It just now occurred.

Operator: Where at?

Caller: We are heading west. We just crossed the summit and this truck was going in the wrong lane. Now the car is on fire.

Operator: Ma'am, what mile marker are you at?

Caller: Um, I can't see one right here. I don't know. We are on the east side of the summit.

Operator: Are you on the eastbound lane?

Caller: We are west bound. This is terrible. The whole front of the car is gone, and it is on fire.

Operator: Is anybody hurt?

Caller: Oh, I'm sure. The truck was going westbound in the eastbound lane.

Operator: Yes.

Caller: I don't know, for about a half mile. We don't know.

Operator: Right, we have him reported. But did he wreck on the eastbound or westbound lane?

Caller: It was on the eastbound lane.

Operator: On the eastbound lane. OK. And you are still east of Snoqualmie Summit?

Caller: Yes. And there are lots and lots of cars that have stopped now. There is a military...

Operator: Two cars involved?

Caller: Yes.

Operator: The black pickup and another passenger car.

Caller: Yes, a blue car.

Operator: OK.

Caller: The man with the fire extinguisher from the National Guard...

Operator: OK, let me get this call in. Can I keep you on the line for a moment?

Audrey had slammed into a car and killed a young girl and her father. A half full bottle of vodka was found on the seat beside her.

So much for controlling the consumption of your alcohol. You'll read this again later in the book "You didn't always get into trouble every time you had been drinking, but whenever you did get into trouble you had been drinking." Mo

Years later, after Audrey got out of prison, she reconciled with the bereaved wife and mother. They wrote a book together entitled "Face To Face." Moderation Management was quick to reject any failure of its moderate drinking plan citing that sixty days before the crash Audrey had resigned from MM (the program she had founded) and joined AA. So the AA program bore the responsibility. Of course, Audrey bore the responsibility.

I simply want to point out the potential hypocrisy of both the "Moderation Camp" and the "Total Abstinence Camp."

The little boy was asked to give the closing prayer after the Sunday School Lesson about the hypocrisy of the Pharisee's.

He offered…

Dear God we thank thee that we are not like those Pharisee's!

AA is soundly criticized for espousing… 1 Drink = 1 Drunk!

My first AA sponsor told me "Mo, as soon as you take that first drink: You Lose Your Vote"

It is true that with just one drink you are "drug affected."

Chapter 3 **Recovery your way!** Is the start of the CAR approach to recovery. The opening idea is that you are in recovery now even if you are still drinking. This doesn't reaffirm the MM moderate drinking view. The point is quickly made that alcohol is no longer your God. Successful recovery leaves clues and with CAR [listen / do / know] you are not stuck in a ditch with a dogma.

 STOPPING DISTANCES

[signs point beyond themselves]

"Awfulizing-Catastrophizing"

They're Rioting in Africa

(Sheldon Harnick /Recorded by The Kingston Trio in 1960)

They're rioting in Africa

They're starving in Spain

There's hurricanes in Florida

And Texas needs rain

———

A Ballad of remorse sung by

Drunk Drivers convicted of Vehicular Homicide:

"I Didn't Know The Gun Was Loaded" (Reprised)

[Hank Fort & Herb Leighton 1949]

I didn't know the gun was loaded

And I'm so sorry my friend

I didn't know the gun was loaded

And I'll never, never do it again!

2

Tender Loving Greed!

Substance Abuse Treatment is in the Doldrums!

The kindest thing I can say about current Substance Abuse Treatment Methodology is that it is dormant and in a very sad spot!

The principle cause of this stagnation is that the profession denies any responsibility for anything, except that they can and will count the beans [capitation] accurately so they can be paid their money!

With an "arrogance of ignorance" they are between ego and ineptitude. They have failed and they lay the blame on the patient for the lack of progress in recovery.

Alcoholism is the only disease I know of that when treatment fails the patient takes all the blame!

An onlooker might easily mistake the majority of counselors as doling out punishment instead of rendering treatment.

The professional training of line counselors is almost none existent and their CEU sessions are often, with justification, called "Teddy Bear Seminars" which leaves them with meager therapy skills. If the only tool you have is a hammer, everybody becomes a nail.

Prior to 1985 most of the treatment for substance abuse was administered at Residential Treatment Facilities. Most of the programs lasted 28 days. Residential treatment was expensive and the expense factor left an opening in the late 1980's for a more economical approach, Intensive Out Patient Treatment. The battle was on for the warm bodies of the abusers and it got nasty. IOP marketers called the residential facilities "Drunk Farms" or worse "Failure Factory's." These liable labels linger to this day.

The sad thing was that at either venue the treatment methodology was lazy. It remains so today. 93% of all these programs "piggy back" with their own version of a "twelve step" treatment program [Dr. Stanton Peele, Reason Magazine, November 2000 issue]. This amounts to a $7 billion a year industry freeloading on the back of Alcoholics Anonymous. Most of this money is paid by insurance companies because the AMA in 1959 declared that alcoholism was a "disease."

There are over 11,000 treatment programs in the USA listed on SAMHSA's (Substance Abuse and Mental Health Services) Treatment Locator.

As a federal bureaucracy all SAMHSA does is print "four color chrome" brochures, proclaim September each year as "National Recovery Month" and dole out one million grant dollars annually, which are easy prey to the crafty grant writer wordsmith!

The most unforgiving aspect of this expenditure of the $7 billion for treatment services by these "Tender Loving Greed" In Patient and Out Patient Bean Counters is that they only "treat" 10% of the 50 million problem drinkers that need help.

In addition there is a "feeding frenzy" for these dollars. With the tough current economic times the "safety net" dollars for substance abuse treatment have been drastically cut. The landscape resembles that at the final watering hole during the dry season on the Serengeti. All animals cluster around, desperate for a drink. In substance abuse treatment the private practices of PhD Psychologists are drying up so they indignantly condescend to push and shove against the hoi polli, competency based journeymen. The competency based counselors are absolutely sure the PhD's know nothing about dealing with substance abuse. I tend to agree with them. These "Two Hatters" have insights as "Wounded Healers" that the hallowed halls of Ivy can't teach. Let's look at the two different treatment "styles."

The "shrinks" use the "slow boat to China" style, not only because the bucks are in the minutes but because "slow boat to China" therapy is based on Freud's "Seduction Theory of Neurosis" i.e. a patient is unable to assimilate the trauma of a past event. Something dreadful and violent and secret happened in their past [e.g. their mother left them in a burning circus] and they have developed "Defense Mechanisms" to cope: e.g. sublimation / projection / paranoia, etc.

With this Treatment the analogy of "The Onion" is often used. You have to peal the onion skin back layer by layer. Always try to find "The Core Defense Mechanism" but Do No Harm! HE DEPENDS ON HIS KEY DEFENSE MECHANISM'S! As a "slow boat to China" Counselor timing and the nature of your delivery are critical. You are dealing with key ADAPTIVE FORCES in a patient's life! Be careful about trying to impose your own! Be Invitational not Confrontational!

The treatment, in the early 1880's, of an Austrian hysteric called Anna O is generally regarded as the beginning of talking-it-through as a form of therapy. But psychoanalysis, as this version of talk therapy became known, is time intensive. Anna's doctor, Josef Breuer, is estimated to have spent over 1,000 hours with her. Sigmund Freud spent an average of 12 hours each day, 6 days a week, in sessions with each of his patients.

The "Two Hatters" are more confrontational almost immediately. Perhaps that's why I've always thrived on the "How To" Recovery Books of Humanist Albert Ellis PhD and proudly claim him as one of my mentors. Ellis was the poster boy for being Confrontational, Invitational was not in his vocabulary. I'll never forget a session with Al when he said simply "Mo you're full of s***." Also Jack Trimpey wrote a courageous book [He took on AA with a vengeance and AA struck back in a rage] "The Small Book" first published in the late eighties [Coincidently Albert Ellis wrote the Introduction]. "The Small Book" planted the first seeds in my early recovery mind that I could be a "thinker" as well as a "believer." That I didn't have to subscribe to a "Ready Guide" cloaked in some Celestial Voice orchestrated by a humanly created Institution. Remember the arrogate bombastic voice of the Wizard of Oz before the curtain was "rent in twain" (this is a tangential reference to Matthew 27:51). In "Pots" and "Bingo" you work directly with God "Panem Ba Panem" "Face to Face" [Job 40:5-6] on your recovery, already in progress. The vesture of Institutional Ordinances are preempted… from now on serving only as helpful views, good to have around but carrying only the weight of suggestions.

There is a very harsh quotation attributed to Saint Augustine when he was speaking of the ills, errors and mistakes of the Church, "The Church is a whore, but she is my mother." This same sentiment honestly applies to the state of both inpatient and outpatient Treatment for alcoholism today "Treatment is a whore, but she is my mother." Many feel it's all we have, but as my first two books [Pots and Bingo] proclaim… we have our own positive selves. We are not powerless over alcohol! We are already in Recovery! A best kept secret about recovery is that it really starts in "aftercare." Aftercare is the key to recovery! Here's our new paradigm:

"Let's Go Big Team… We want some ACTION!

Two Hatters
Wounded Healers

Dr. Bob gives us our "Mission Statement" in six words:

"Trust God Clean House Help Others"

Our "New Battle Strategy" is outlined right now as I call a Special Meeting of The Secret Mission Club...

 STOPPING DISTANCES

[signs point beyond themselves]

The Secret Mission Club
Special Meeting

Two Secret Battle Strategies
From
Two Super Duper Generals
For
Two Hatters Everywhere

I Call this meeting to order... here is the strategy...

[For the background of "The Secret Mission Club" including its origin and early secret missions see the "As Memory Serves Me" Radio Script p.xvii]

- No 5¢ dues for this meeting only.
- No spitting on the floor or writing on the walls... will still be enforced.
- I brought chocolate chips for our snack.

This is the most important meeting of The Secret Mission Club in 50 years. 50 years ago we "conquered" Mr. Thompson [our town atheist who would eat people then rake leaves] because of our secret "Tactics" that nobody else had even thought of.

Today we have new "Tactics" because we have a new and tougher enemy. I call them "The People of the Lie" and they are real sneaky because they wear sheep outfits like the Bible talks about. They make lots of money selling us "Tender Loving Greed."

Our two new Super Duper "Tactics" are:

1. Operation Cartwheel (1943-1944).

   General Douglas MacArthur was ready to fulfill his promise "I shall return" and the Japanese knew it. They had loaded up every Island, even the smallest with tons of cannons and mad men with guns and barbed wire and stuff. The same sort of thing we all do in "Monopoly" when some poor victim is about to turn the corner and head toward our "Green Property" Lair...

   - Pennsylvania Avenue/Rent: Hotel $1,400
   - Japanese Type 92 70 MM Infantry Gun/Rent: Many many Dead US Marines

   MacArthur took a look and said "No Way!" He made the very wise decision of Cart Wheeling (Hop Scotching) over the: Pacific Avenue / North Carolina Avenue / Pennsylvania Avenue Islands of the Solomon Chain [e.g. Kavieng, Kolombangara and Rabaul]

   Pay attention...we'll use this same tactic!

2. "Millennium Challenge" (2002) Retired "Old Foggy" General Paul Van Riper defeated the entire US Military in what was supposed to be the definitive "War Game."

   Instead, shortly after "The Games" began they had to be cancelled, because they ["The Blue Forces"] had LOST!

Van Riper immediately at the "starting gun" unleashed an arsenal of unorthodox tactics. He knew, this "Grand Show" was being staged to justify the impending attack on Iraq and that all the War Lord's chatter was about "the flavor of the day" a "Preemptive" strike. So he thought a preempt of the preempt was the thing to do. He used motorcycle messengers to communicate instead of using expensive microwave communications. He used row boats powered by small Johnson Outboard Motors to ram and sink Guided Missile Destroyers. These little putt putts sank 16 "Blue Force" ships, most of the US expeditionary fleet. If "The Games" had really happened, it would have been the worst naval disaster since Pearl Harbor! Almost instantly, the 250 million dollars spent in the prep of the "Blue Forces" went down the drain. It took just one day of "combat."

The red faced Pentagon top brass had to pretend that the whole thing had never happened. The dead troops of the "Blue Forces" came back to life and the sunken fleet resurfaced again.

How did this happen? **Van Riper kept it simple...**

3

Recovery your way!

To borrow an expression from Saint Augustine, your "Ordo del Amoris" is changing!

That is, your "**Order of Loves**" is changing!

The following transparent analogy will help clarify the process:

Let's pretend that the love of your life is Ethyl. [Note: In the female version, the love of your life is Jack.] As a professional woman, she travels a lot and there are many tearful departures at airports. But the knowledge is always there that she will return. Then one day the news arrives that Ethyl's plane has crashed and she is dead. There is a funeral and the painful grieving process of closure begins.

This is where you are in recovery . . . right now! You are standing at the graveside, throwing dirt on Ethyl Alcohol. (In the female version, you are throwing dirt on Jack Daniel's from Lynchburg, Tenn.) You know now that alcohol can no longer be the love of your life! There is a big hole right in the middle of your stomach that, in the past, only Ethyl Alcohol or Jack Daniel's could fill. What, if anything, can take her/his place? [Important note: You never "break a habit or an addiction"; you do put something else in its place.]

Stay calm, be patient! Patience is so difficult for an obsessive compulsive alcoholic personality ("I want what I want when I want it . . . I don't want pain, I want relief . . . now!"), but it is necessary!

Changing suitors is confusing. The manipulation is immense. We've all gone through it. In fact, most of us have been on both sides of the scenario:

The plea: "Honey, just take me back this one last time, and I promise I'll never do wrong again!"

The response: "You've said that before!"

The plea: "I know I have, but this time it will be different!"

Alcohol is the master of all the ploys. "How it works" (from chapter five of THE BIG BOOK, read at the start of every AA meeting) gets it exactly right. In that reading are these words of caution: "Remember, we deal with alcohol, cunning, baffling, powerful . . . ." Why is this apparently innocuous liquid, a source of pleasure and humor for so many, the source of misery and despair for us? Just listen to this story:

MALARKEY: "I WILL NOT BE MOVED!"

The debate had been loud and hostile. Finally, the Politician rose to speak. The room grew silent.

"If by Alcohol you mean, 'That devil's brew that rents asunder friendships, jobs and families, that inebriating toxin that brings previously noble men and women to the brink of despair and desperation. That pickling polluted malt that causes weeping little babies to be dragged away from their hopeless, swaggering father's. If that, my friends, is what you mean by Alcohol . . . then I am against it with all my heart. This is my stand . . . I will not be moved!

But if by Alcohol, you mean, 'That marvelous social elixir that builds warm friendships and happy times at social gatherings throughout our land, that steamy, hot toddy that once again puts the spring back into an old codger's step on a cold winter's morning, that cool thirst quencher, the income from which fills the coffers of the local schools so our youth of tomorrow can be educated and have a chance to live their dreams!' If that, my friends, is what you mean by

Alcohol . . . then I am for it with all my heart. This is my stand . . . I will not be moved!"

At this point one of the fundamental rules of all good public speakers applies to you:

When you're in a hurry, skip everything . . .
BUT THE PAUSES!

Here's a necessary and important pause. We are going to do a thorough post mortem of the deceased. The last thing we need (just when we thought the horror was over) is a Jason-like "Halloween movie . . . alcoholic hand," sticking itself out of the ground, beckoning us back!

AN AUTOPSY OF ALCOHOL

Chemists disparagingly call Alcohol a stupid molecule (how right they are). AA Members fearfully call Alcohol "Cunning, Baffling and Powerful." Those are two very divergent views.

Let's take a look and see how both views are absolutely correct. The Chemists are talking about the very simple nature of Alcohol's molecular structure C_2H_5OH It looks like this:

To a spine of two carbon atoms are attached five hydrogen atoms and a hydroxyl (oxygen-hydrogen):

$$H - \overset{\overset{\displaystyle H}{|}}{\underset{\underset{\displaystyle H}{|}}{C}} - \overset{\overset{\displaystyle H}{|}}{\underset{\underset{\displaystyle H}{|}}{C}} - OH$$

Ether is Alcohol without "the chaser." Its molecular structure is not similar it's <u>exactly the same</u> without the hydroxyl (OH Water). Ether is in fact a compound obtained from Alcohol by the introduction and interaction of Sulfuric Acid.

You wouldn't conceive of attempting to crawl off the operating table after being sedated, stagger out the door to your car and drive home; and yet you would not hesitate to do the same thing when blowing at or near a .08 into an alcohol intoximeter.

 **WORD: NATURE OR NURTURE?**

This is as good a time as any to deal with the argument of genetic addiction to alcohol. It's unbelievable to me that so many books have been written and so much precious recovery time lost arguing about "nature or nurture." As a thesis topic, it's gotten some counselors their PhDs, and in group therapy sessions, it's allowed some group members to avoid accepting the responsibility for their own drinking problem. I used to call group diversion topics like this "chasing rabbits" or "gnawing on the bone" or "navel gazing."

The research seems to indicate that about 8% of all alcoholics have a genetic predisposition for the disease of alcoholism. I am not egotistical enough to believe that I qualify for this special group, although I had Uncles on both sides of my family that were genuine alcoholics. **Like all the remaining 92% of us, I had to really work at becoming an alcoholic.** But I'm here to proclaim that I, just like you, have succeeded! If you quack like a duck and walk like a duck … you're a duck!

Note: Alcoholism is the only disease that you get yelled at for having. You don't hear, "Damn it, Mo, you're a hopeless Diabetic!"

 SMOKER: ABOUT AVOIDING RESPONSIBILITY!

Do you remember this "Peanuts" comic strip?

Lucy was running around to all her friends and asking them to sign a piece of paper. She would confront each one and say:

"Sign this, it absolves me from all blame."

They would sign it and with a quick "thank you" she was off to get another signature. Finally, as fate would have it, she came to Charlie Brown. He signed as she requested, and as she walked away Lucy said:

"No matter what happens any place or any time in the world this absolves me from all blame and responsibility."

As the cartoon ends, Charlie Brown is standing there looking puzzled and saying:

"That must be a nice document to have."

PUT THAT IN YOUR PIPE AND SMOKE IT!

MALARKEY: THE UNDERLYING MYTHOLOGY:

"I CAN HANDLE IT!"

An alcoholic was undergoing a physical examination. When his doctor requested that he hold out his arm at full length, he did so and his hand shook wildly.

The doctor asked, "Are you still drinking a lot?"

Still shaking, the patient responded "I've cut way down. I don't drink a third of what I use to. I spill most of it!"

Cecil C.

Alcohol allows a person to substitute the pleasant for the unpleasant. You drink booze because it makes you feel good!

Alcohol is a chemical composed of Carbon, Hydrogen, and Oxygen.

$$C_2H_5OH$$

("Better things for better living through chemistry" [DuPont])

Alcohol is oxidized (burned up by the liver) at the rate of ¾ of an ounce an hour.

Alcohol is a sedative drug and Alcoholism is addiction to that drug!

It works inside the brain. First, it makes a rush for the brain's pleasure circuit. Activating this circuit (i.e., releasing the neurotransmitters dopamine and serotonin, which govern our sense of well being, as well as other opioids) makes you feel good! The rent's still due and the marriage is still in shambles, but you don't care anymore!

You feel euphoric, talkative and excited!

As your blood-alcohol level continues to rise, alcohol remains busy, anesthetizing the remaining neurons in the ventral tegmentum that connect with the pleasure center. It goes deeper, flipping off switches in areas that affect the voluntary brain functions: thought (the cortex), movement (cerebellum), and emotion (amygdala).

At this point, with any luck, you pass out. If too much alcohol is consumed and not metabolized, the involuntary brain functions (heartbeat and breathing) stop . . . **and you die!!**

It's important to realize that this process is the same for anyone and everyone who consumes alcohol. So what is the difference between the "Normal" drinker and the "Alcoholic?"

Alcohol opens the neurotransmitter floodgates. Chronic use produces lasting changes. As human beings, we are primarily comprised of chemicals and electrical charges. This is never truer than in the synapses of the brain, that marvelous bowl of vegetable soup where nerve impulses via neurotransmitters and receptors "play ball" with each other. The pitchers (transmitters) throw the ball to the catchers (receptors). In an alcohol-affected brain, the catchers soon get worn out trying to catch so many hot and wild fast balls. Exhaustion or injury wipes them out. Now the problem starts for the chronic drinker. An unintended consequence kicks in. Because there are fewer catchers' mitts available to catch those pleasurable fast balls, the game isn't as much fun any more! This is the molecular basis for tolerance!

The same amount of alcohol doesn't have the same pleasure-producing effect that it originally did.

Note: This is when "chasing the high" begins!

What's even worse is that with fewer pleasure pitches being caught, everything in life seems to be impotent! The only escape from irritability, anxiety, and depression is to drink more and more booze!

In the beginning, drinking alcohol was about feeling good! But addiction is about avoiding total despair!

Recovery begins when you realize this!

The Ethyl / Jack you once knew is dead!

The "Good News" is that "A Match . . . The Match . . . Made In Heaven" is waiting!
Realization that you are changing is critical!

Oliver Wendell Holmes said, "Man's mind stretched to a new idea never goes back to its original dimensions." You are in the process of breaking out of a vicious cycle of self-defeating behavior. You no longer worship a false god! Paul Tillich, the great Protestant theologian, defined **God** as **"that to which you give your ultimate dependence."** You now know you can no longer ultimately depend on alcohol to solve or mask life's problems, or, more simply, be your best friend! In fact, alcohol **itself** has become . . . the enemy . . . the <u>problem</u>!

Before this starts to feel like it's becoming the complicated verse in the hymn book, let's put a "Band Aid" cure in place for those tempting "even if you are still drinking" episodes. The "Band Aid" comes in the form of a song and is your first assignment! The song is about Finnegan, the Irish leprechaun who's been hanging out in the margins.

Assignment #1

With my Irish heritage (County Claire by the river Shannon) [Note: alcoholism has been called "the Irish allergy"], when other kids were singing the round, "10 Little Indians," to the same tune I was singing:

FINNEGAN BEGIN AGAIN

You can find the sheet music for this in the appendix;
Take the time to learn it by heart, now:

There was an old man named Michael Finnegan.
He grew whiskers on his chin again.
He shaved them off but they grew back in again.
Poor old Michael Finnegan begin again!

This little song, this little gimmick, will give you the **courage to be,** just when you are sure that, once again, you and your vodka bottle are lower than a footprint!

Apply it to your wound immediately! It will help ease the pain in this critical early stage of recovery. In time it will shift from being a gimmick to being a **powerful recovery tool!**

Martin Luther said that the devil hates to hear a Christian singing. In the same way, Ethyl Alcohol hates to hear a sober alcoholic singing!

Remembering this childhood refrain in one of the very deepest, darkest days of my drinking history literally saved my life. In the days, weeks, and months that followed, sometimes after climbing once again out of the vodka bottle, I could hardly get the words out. The cadence was almost mournful, similar to the way Barbara Streisand sings "Happy Days Are Here Again." Other times, when faced with the standard variety of daily problems that used to devastate me and "drive me to drink" (the "ain't got the money for the mortgage on the farm" type of problem) my tempo and vitality would, amazingly, be pretty much up to my age seven level of enthusiasm. Finnegan was always there, ready to begin again! Being a victim, feeling sorry for myself, were no longer options!

Woody Hayes, the famous Ohio State football coach, was once asked what football taught his student athletes. Woody replied, "Football teaches you that when you get knocked down, **you get back up!**" Recovery teaches the same thing and more: you not only get back up . . . **you begin again!**

You now have the ability to take action!

 **SMOKER: ABOUT BEING A VICTIM!**

Do you remember this episode in "Calvin and Hobbes"?

Calvin was philosophizing and he reasoned that whenever he does something wrong, it is not really his fault. Society is to blame. Here is how he put it:

"Nothing I do is my fault. My family is dysfunctional."

"And my parents won't empower me! Consequently, I am not self-actualized."

"My behavior is addictive, functioning in a diseased process of toxic co-dependency."

"I need holistic healing and wellness before I will accept any responsibility for my actions."

How well I remember, in the height of my denial days, being a card-carrying member of the "culture of victimhood"!

PUT THAT IN YOUR PIPE AND SMOKE IT!

And while we're here, let's have some fun listening to these "victims" gender bash:

"If only I had shot him when I first met him!"

"It serves me right for putting all my eggs in one bastard!" Dorothy Parker

"Whatever women do they must do twice as well as men to be thought half as good. Luckily, this is not difficult." Charlotte Whitton

"I am a doormat in a world of boots." Jean Rhys

"From my experience of life I believe my personal motto should be, 'Beware of men bearing flowers.'" Muriel Spark

"He taught me housekeeping; when I divorce I keep the house." Zsa Zsa Gabor

"Women deprived of the company of men pine; men deprived of the company of women become stupid." Anonymous

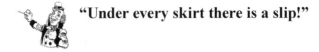 **"Under every skirt there is a slip!"**

"Women's Rights are men's duties." Karl Kraus

"When a man steals your wife, there is no better revenge then to let him keep her." Sacha Guitry

"There is one thing women can never take away from men. We die sooner." P.J. O'Rourke

"The female sex has no greater fan than I, and I have the bills to prove it." Alan Jay Lerner

What's important here is that you eliminate such thoughts of "victimhood." No longer are you going to view yourself as a victim of your love.

Remember, **you are changing your "Ordo del Amoris" from alcohol to God, and He's not going to make you a victim!**

On this note, I've always found it helpful to remember lines from Francis Thompson's poem "The Hound of Heaven." As the speaker implies, all of us have "fled Him, down the nights and down the days [. . .] fled Him, down the arches of the years." But then God says,

> All which I took from thee I did but take,
> Not for thy harms,
> But just that thou might'st seek it in My arms,
> All which thy child's mistake
> Fancies as lost, I have stored for thee at home:
> Rise, clasp My hand, and come!

 STOPPING DISTANCES

[signs point beyond themselves]

Phineas and You...

["Every drink you drink is <u>potentially</u> spiked." Mo]

The most often disputed aspect of this CAR "Recovery Model" is the declaration that "you are in recovery even if you are still drinking." I'm not going to re litigate that contention here. However, I will never deny that a very real danger does exist when you pick up even one drink! Whenever you take a drink there is a possibility that you will modulate from being a Finnegan (Begin Your Recovery Again)...a moderator of "correct" behavior; to being a "Spiked through the head" <u>Phineas</u>.

Before "the accident" Phineas had been able to inhibit inappropriate behavior and initiate appropriate behavior. Everybody loved him. He was kind, courteous and always friendly. Then the accident happened:

On September 13, 1848 twenty-five year old Phineas Gage was a construction supervisor for the Rutland and Burlington Railroad. They were laying new track. He was in charge of adding blasting powder into holes bored in rock, adding a fuse and tamping everything down with a six foot "spike' (tamping rod). At 4:30 pm on that day the powder exploded when he "tamped" and the spike / rod went through his head (see picture). Amazingly he survived and seemed for all intents and purposes as normal as before. But he wasn't. The damage to his frontal lobes made him fitful, irreverent, obstinate, impatient, indulging at times in the grossest profanity, uncaring for his fellow workers. Phineas' well balanced mind was gone. Friends commented that he "was no longer Gage." [Recovery from the Passage of an Iron Bar through the Head, John M. Harlow, M.D. 1869]

Each drink of alcohol potentially carries the same "spike" and same damage. It can equally devastate the same pre frontal lobes of <u>your</u> cortex.

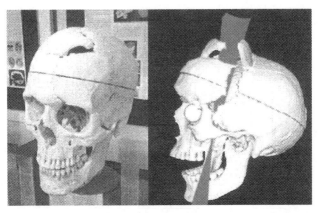

Harvard Medical Museum

Yep... some of my hangovers felt exactly like that! Mo

As memory
serves me
By Mo Murray
Friendly recollections of people, places and events
in the not-too-distant past.

Puzzles

When was the last time you put together a jigsaw puzzle? My older sister and I did a lot of them when we were kids. Which prompts me to take a moment to look at both the Puzzle and the Puzzlee.

First, the Puzzle. You dump what seems like 542,000 pieces on the card table and start to sort them out. Generally, you wind up with three distinct piles – a sky blue pile, a sickly-looking bluish-black pile, and a definitely black pile.

Now, let's look at the puzzlee. Here there are two classic types – the zappers and the turners.

The zappers are exemplified by my older sister. They grab a piece laying upside down halfway across the table and ZAP! – in it goes.

The turners are exemplified by yours truly. We are definitely more stylish, but dumber. We pick up an interesting looking piece with one big knob and three small ones and turn it, and turn it... and turn it. Somehow I'm reminded of the disclaimer that flashes on the screen after one of the TV quiz shows. It says in effect: "The quick recall of specific facts is not necessarily a measure of overall intelligence." I don't really believe that, but as vice-president of the society of slow thinkers, I'm grateful it's there.

I guess one of the finest justifications for the reflective approach to life is found in Sherlock Holmes. Mr. Holmes' attraction – it seems – is not the fact that he solves the crime immediately, but that at the outset he understands more of the mystery.

Now that we have the puzzle workers identified, let's take a closer look at those three piles of pieces.

I like to think the pretty blue pile of puzzle pieces exemplifies all the happy and beautiful things in our lives. Let's hope we all have our share of those. But, even so, we tend to bolster them a bit with carpeting in our latest set of wheels, or some new graphite-shafted golf clubs.

Which seems to be leading us into the bluish-black pile, doesn't it? Things aren't always so beautiful here. One of society's answers to this is the "How To" craze. No matter what you want to be, there's probably a book that'll tell you "How To" be just that, Ira Wallach has satirized this phenomenon in his book "How To BE Deliriously Happy"…which such chapter headings as "Seizing the Ceasar in Yourself," and "How To Change the Indigestible You Into the Savory Self."

Finally, the black pile doesn't need much explanation. We don't have to be reminded of the many tragedies we face in and around our lives. But, before we get too gloomy, let me merely make this point: Whether we're zappers or a turner, we still have to make all the pieces fit together.

4

God fixes cracked pots!

(Jeremiah 18:1-6)

1. The word which came to Jeremiah from the Lord, saying,
2. Arise, and go down to the potter's house, and there I will cause thee to hear my words.
3. Then I went down to the potter's house, and, behold, he wrought a work on the wheels.
4. And the vessel that he made of clay was marred in the hands of the potter: so he made it again another vessel, as seemed good to the potter to make *it*.
5. Then the word of the Lord came to me saying,
6. [Alcoholic], cannot I do with you as this potter? saith the Lord. Behold, as the clay *is* in the potter's hand, so *are* ye in mine hand, O [Alcoholic].

(Jeremiah 18:1-6)
(KJV / My Inserts)

I know you're anxious, but once again, you need to be **patient**. You're not going to get anywhere until you get an attitude change.

ASSIGNMENT #2

WRITE AN ESSAY, IN 500 WORDS OR LESS,

(Note: Just like in Senior English)

ON THE TOPIC:

"HOW TO MAKE YOURSELF ABSOLUTELY MISERABLE!"

Why engage in such a negative exercise?

Once you are aware of self-defeating behavior, you can change it!

Two expressions from the rooms of AA come to mind:

"Keep It Green!"

"Look back over your shoulder, but don't stare!"

You are writing this as the expert! Remember to emphasize the things you learned in class:

Awfulize: Make things as bad as possible!

Catastrophize: If possible, bring in the looming disasters of global warming, the hole in the ozone layer, and the disappearance of our clean water supply!

Triangulate: There is no problem so perfect that it can't be split up and made into three equally wonderful problems!

Emphasize Terminal Uniqueness: Nobody knows the trouble you've known!

I was always most successful in making myself absolutely miserable late on a gloomy Sunday afternoon. Even before my drinking days, I would get nostalgic on Sunday afternoons. All I had to add was vodka and the isolation (isolation is always helpful) of my darkened bedroom! Just like that I could turn nostalgia into melancholy (from the Greek word meaning "black bile"). It also helps to lie on your bed and stare at the ceiling!

Active alcoholics are master "self-manipulators." They are the last ones to acknowledge and relinquish their deceptions.

 **MALARKEY: THINKING LIKE AN ALCOHOLIC:**

SELECTIVE PERCEPTION!

A man walked into his doctor's office and announced, "Doc, you've got to help my friends! I'm dead but none of them believe me!"

The doctor diagnosed the situation and advised his patient, "Go home and every morning for one week, stand in front of your bathroom mirror, stare at yourself, and repeat over and over again, 'Dead men don't bleed!'"

The man left and one week later returned to the doctor's office. The doctor asked, "Now, every morning did you stand in front of your mirror and repeat, 'Dead men don't bleed?'"

"Yes, Doctor," came the reply. At which time the doctor picked up a scalpel and jabbed the man in his right thumb.

As blood spurted out, the amazed man stared down at his thumb and exclaimed, **"What do you know . . . dead men do bleed!"**

WORD: THINKING LIKE AN EARTH PERSON:
PERCEPTION IS REALITY!

Is this a young lady or an old woman? *created by British cartoonist W.E. Hill, Punk Humor Magazine, 1915.

I love this story from Carl Sandburg's "The People, Yes." It says it all about perception:

> Who was that early sodbuster in Kansas? He leaned at the gatepost and studied the horizon and figured what corn might do next year and tried to calculate why God ever made the grasshopper and why two days of hot winds smother the life out of a stand of wheat and why there was such a spread between what he got for grain and the price quoted in Chicago and New York. Drove up a newcomer in a covered wagon: "What kind of folks live around here?" "Well, stranger, what kind of folks was there in the country

you come from?" "Well, they was mostly a lowdown, lying, thieving, gossiping, backbiting lot of people." "Well, I guess, stranger, that's about the kind of folks you'll find around here." And the dusty gray stranger had just about blended into the dusty gray cottonwoods in a clump on the horizon when another newcomer drove up. "What kind of folks live around here?" "Well, stranger, what kind of folks was there in the country you come from?" "Well, they was a mostly a decent, hardworking, lawabiding, friendly lot of people." "Well, I guess, stranger, that's about the kind of folks you'll find around here." And the second wagon moved off and blended with the dusty cottonwoods on the horizon while the early sodbuster leaned at his gatepost and tried to figure why two days of hot winds smother the life out of a nice stand of wheat.

This next one is "sick," but I like it, too:

A monk entered a monastery noted for its code of silence. The only time he was allowed to speak was once every twenty years when he met with the Abbot. At that time he was only allowed to say two words.

After twenty years the monk met with the Abbot and the Abbot said:
"My child, you can speak your two words."

He responded with these two words:
"Bed hard."

After twenty more years of silence, he met with the Abbot again and was invited to speak his two words. He said:

WORD: CHANGE YOUR ATTITUDE AND

YOU WILL CHANGE YOUR LIFE!

John Milton in Paradise Lost wrote it this way "The mind is its own place, and in itself can make a heaven of hell, a hell of heaven."

Here's one of the very best examples of making heaven of hell:

In his book Man's Search For Meaning, Viktor Frankl recalls the horrors of life and death in Auschwitz, a Nazi concentration camp. As well as recalling the suffering, hunger, cold, and brutality, he writes these words:

> We who lived in concentration camps can remember the men who walked through the huts comforting others, giving away their last pieces of bread. They may have been few in number, but they offer suffcient proof that everything can be taken from a man but one thing: the last of human freedoms — **to choose one's attitude in any given set of circumstances**, to choose one's own way.
>
> Victor Frankl
>
> (Emphasis mine)

Attitude

By

Charles Swindoll

The longer I live, the more I realize the impact of attitude on life. Attitude, to me, is more important than facts. It is more important than the past, than education, than money, than circumstances, than failures, than successes, than what other people think or say or do. It is more important than appearance, giftedness or skill. It will make or break a company . . . a church . . . a home. The remarkable thing is we have a choice every day regarding the attitude we will embrace for that day. We cannot change our past . . . we cannot change the fact that people will act in a certain way. We cannot change the inevitable. The only thing we can do is play on the one string we have, and that is our attitude . . . I am convinced that life is 10% what happens to me and 90% how I react to it. And so it is with you . . . we are in charge of our attitudes.

ASSIGNMENT #3:
This time you are the expert with a "positive attitude."

With trusty pencil in hand, start writing a new type of "**Gratitude Journal**." I don't want you to just generally write down, as they come to mind, the things you are grateful for. This approach is too vague. At the top of the page write:

To have what you want, want what you have!

Here's how it works:

I WANT: I wish I had one of those great big old luxury cars, yeah . . . a big, shiny, black, four-door Cadillac Brougham. About a 1989 model with all the bells and whistles but none of that pollution control stuff!

I HAVE: I have one of those great big old luxury cars. It's a big, shiny, black, four-door Cadillac Brougham. It's a 1989 model with all the bells and whistles but none of that pollution control stuff! It was my father's. I got it when he died. We spent long hours driving in it together. We still do!

It's not so much a gratitude journal as an expanded "**thank you list**." It's so much fun! When you're done you'll really be pumped up! You'll be cheering as if you were back at one of your old high school football pep rallies. That beats standard government-issue gratitude by a whole lot!

This is the reverse of being allowed to get rid of all your problems by putting them on a table at the front of an auditorium full of people. Everyone else in attendance is invited to do the same thing and by the time the last person has "dumped," you run forward as fast as you can, hoping you are able to reclaim your "woes" before someone else grabs them!

These words from Desiderata are a great "attitude adjuster."

Go placidly amid the noise and haste,
and remember what peace there may be in silence.
As far as possible without surrender
be on good terms with all persons.
Speak your truth quietly and clearly;
and listen to others,
even the dull and ignorant;
they too have their story.

In many ways, the most important thing in early recovery is to pay attention to details! Here are some words from my idol and golfing mentor since 1948, Ben Hogan (I just had to get this in some place):

> It may seem that we have gone into unwarranted detail about the elements of the correct grip. This is anything but the case. Too often in golf, players mistake the generality for the detail. [. . .] **In golf there are certain things you must do quite precisely, where being approximately right is not right enough**.
>
> (Emphasis mine)
>
> In the same way,

Too often in recovery, players mistake the generality for the detail. **In recovery there are certain things you must do quite precisely, where being approximately right is:**

not right enough!

Bill Wilson, Co-Founder of AA, said it this way: **"The Good is too often the enemy of the best!"**

Here's an example:

For years, as a substance abuse counselor, I had on my desk the sign, "IF NOTHING CHANGES / NOTHING CHANGES!" It seemed both clever and profound. However, like so much information in this field, filed with myths and fallacies, it was a half-truth, i.e., **not right enough!** Let's acknowledge the insightful side of this "slogan" by recounting its most widely told yarn:

A man climbs the steps to the fourth floor of a building. He runs down the hall and jumps out the window, falling down to the pavement below, breaking his right leg. He then pulls himself back up the steps and repeats the process. This time he breaks his left leg. The sequence is repeated until the man is completely immobilized.

At this point the storyteller suggests a definition of insanity: *Doing the same thing over and over again and expecting a different result!* This is an accurate snapshot of the negative consequences of compulsive drinking in the life of a problem drinker.

My father used another one of his aviation analogies to describe me and my dilemma: "Son, you're like a test pilot who keeps putting his plane into a dive to see if the wings will come off." I like his comparison better. It pictures an **action**, however chaotic, and reveals the half-truth nature of the "leap to the parking lot" story. Story #1 is fixed and two-dimensional. It's like the Greek myth of Sisyphus, whom the gods condemned to roll a large rock to the top of a mountain, watch the rock tumble back down to the bottom, and repeat the process endlessly.

Story #1 suggests that the "alcoholic" has a preference for futile suffering. The whole life of an active alcoholic is seen as being exerted toward accomplishing nothing.

In Story #2, however, **revolt, defined as a counteraction,** and **not** denial, can be seen to be the motivating force.

I've spent my fair share of time in treatment on "drunk farms" and on the various psychiatric floors of hospitals. With and without the influence of heavy medication, I was known to defiantly pronounce: "You don't tie an elephant to a tree!"

In a horrifying way, I was recalling an incident I saw on a National Geographic Special. It still makes me cringe every time I remember it! Elephant trainers in India would tie a stubborn elephant to a tree for days, weeks, and if necessary months, until the spirit of the terrorized beast was broken! Sadly, far too many substance abuse counselors in the "treatment community" need to get the message:

You don't tie an elephant to a tree!

And while we're at it, here are a few other considerations for counselors to keep in mind:

* Martin Luther said that, preaching the Gospel of Jesus Christ was like pouring milk through a sack of coal! Counselors do the same thing with God's recovery message to the alcoholic.

* "If the only treatment tool you have is a hammer, everybody becomes a nail!" (Mo)

* "Before you can walk in another person's shoes, you must first take off your own!" (Mo)

My argument here is not, as it might seem, with semantics. It is with the "treatment community's" inflexible notion that submission is the key to "fixing" the alcoholic! At the same time, the alcoholic, by desperately clinging to **revolt** as a survival technique (albeit a mere shoestring of one) retains **energy**! Through his own eyes, the possibility of death through drinking is recognized! By refusing "resignation," the struggle to restore the dignity to his life remains an option.

This does not imply an innate benefit from continuing to "road test" with alcohol. However, "denial" should more fairly be called an alcoholic's "Ethic of Renunciation." In a real way, denial restores the majesty of life to an alcoholic!

Here's the key: Even as the carnage of futile leaps and death spirals continues, the "Ah-Ha experience" (to use the expression of the psychologist William James) of understanding and acknowledgement is in progress! These creative moments cannot be legislated! The old adage ("If nothing changes, nothing changes"), perfectly true, but so often ignored through an alcoholic haze, is now being seriously considered as periods of sobriety stretch from days to weeks to months.

John Bradshaw is an excellent counselor. Here's his skillful summation:

Anger is your dignity emotion and you don't have energy if you don't have dignity!"

So much for trees and elephants. **Remember . . . Ethyl Alcohol <u>is dead!</u>**

And you are changing your attitude!

As memory serves me
By Mo Murray
Friendly recollections of people, places and events
in the not-too-distant past.

The Real Gift

What do you remember about your early years as a philanthropist. O.K., pardon the high-fallutin word. What I'm really asking is: What do you recall about the gifts you gave us a child?

Now, be honest. I bet you haven't given as much of yourself in a gift as when you gave your Dad that hand-painted rock as a paperweight for his desk. Or when you presented your Mother with that made-all-by-yourself letter holder . . . you know – the crayoned paper plates laced together with bright yellow ribbon and you delivered it with a kiss.

But, as we grow up, we can lose some of that original gift-giving spirit. And this can happen for a number of reasons.

First, we get introduced to our modern medium of exchange – money. All of a sudden, we kids started getting allowances and saving a few pennies here and there. Now that's all well and good. But then we announced that for Auntie Alice's birthday we wanted to buy her a present. Right away some of that personal touch starts to slip away.

The next gift-giving influence we kids came across was competition. I guess it's the children's version of "keeping ahead of the Joneses." But it hit home with me at a children's birthday party not too long ago when one little girl announced to another: "My present costs more than yours."

The final factor that comes into play is time. How often as adults we rush around the day before a special occasion and buy some indistinguishable knick-knack and send it off with a hurriedly-written greeting.

Now, my idea of the real gift-giver is Cyrus the Great. He was a Greek that was immortalized by Xenophon. You see, Xenophon explained that if Cyrus drank some particularly good wine, he would send the half-empty bottle to a friend with this message: "Cyrus says that he has not tasted better wine than this for a long time, so he gives the rest to you, asking only that you enjoy it today with friends you love the best." How's that for thoughtfulness?

Or Cyrus would send half a goose instructing the messenger to say: "Cyrus has enjoyed this immensely and wants you also to savor of it." Xenophon concludes that Cyrus was the one man among all men who really knew how to give a gift. I'm sure you agree.

Cyrus the Great has been gone over a thousand years now. But just over a hundred years ago Ralph Waldo Emerson – that sage of Concord, Massachusetts – summed it up beautifully. Emerson expressed the same spirit you and I had when we crayoned those yellow flowers on the paper plates for our Moms. Or painted the rock paperweights for our Dads. For, as memory serves me, Emerson said it all in these few words: "The only real gift is a portion of thyself."

 STOPPING DISTANCES

[Memorize these. They <u>will</u> be on the written portion of your exam]

[signs point beyond themselves]

"Problem Drinkers" are a vital ingredient in the "Substance Abuse Industry."

"THE BOOZE BUSINESS"

They support these vocations:

Distillers and Brewers

Distributors

Residential Treatment Facilities

Intensive Out Patient Centers

Detox Units

Counselors

Psychologist

Psychiatrist

Physicians, Nurses & Staff

Researchers

Farmers [growing grains that ferment, malt] (not including dandelion wine)

Government Agencies (Federal and State) NIAAA, SAMSA, NCADD, etc

Professional and Trade Associations

Pharmaceutical Companies and Drug Sales Reps (Naltrexone, Vivtrol, Anti Depressants)

Self Help Authors and Publishers

Book Stores

Law enforcement

Prisons and Jails

Correction Officers

Social Workers

Non-profits (e.g. MADD)

5

The chair's fixed, relax and sit in it!

"Beginning Again" reflects the fact that **recovery is a process**, not an event. In the rooms of Alcoholics Anonymous, I was not what was known as a "one white chip miracle." I could fill a dresser drawer with all my "beginning again" white chips. I was and am today, truly, a recovery work in progress. For you, right now, the earliest phase of this process has begun.

 **GROW UP OR THROW UP:
"TRUST THE PROCESS"**

Note: The phrase "trust the process" makes even me want to throw up! It has turned into a "thought cliché" that weakens attention and no longer starts thought! Here's what I mean by "process" as it relates to recovery from alcohol abuse:

During World War II, there was a British Training Manual about the wartime building of airplanes. It contained a statement to this effect:

> Those who are best at the overall planning and building of airplanes are those who realize that overall planning and building of airplanes by one directorate is quite impossible, and plan for it!

(The Commemorative Air Force, Tuskeegee
Airmen Annual Reunion, Orlando, ca. 1985)

If you scoff that that is typically British, here's the American equivalent. It was heard in rural bus stops throughout the USA for years:

"Last call for the bus to (let's say) Recoveryville! All those wanting to board the bus should already be on the bus!"

John Calvin had a predestined spiritual version of the recovery process:

"Before you were born you were chosen!"

Likewise, Paul Tillich said that Christianity is "Accepting your acceptance!"

Note: This sounds very much like the short form of the first 3 steps of AA:

Step #1: I can't!
Step #2: He can!
Step #3: I think I'll let Him!

Unfortunately, the recovery process is not a straight line up!

I've already reassured you that you are in recovery now . . . So, to go with your new song, you get **a new name!**

You are no longer a noun (I.E. "ALCOHOLIC"), of a class of words denoting a person, place or thing.

You, Recovering Lady, Samantha, or, Recovering Man, Samuel, are **verbs,** defined as any class of words expressing action, existence, or occurrence. In your case, **you are existence with a "big jigger" of . . . action!**

SAMANTHAING and SAMUELING!

This is very bad English, but great recovery!

Now it gets even better!

God felt the same way about Himself. Pay attention to how God pulls this one off!

Moses: Who shall I say sent me?
God: I am who I am! Tell them I am sent you!
(Exodus 3:13-14)

That's: יהוה

A form of the verb "to be": הוה

Therefore, God also is a verb!

The really better part is that both you and God are transitive verbs. Transitive verbs require a direct object ("DO") to complete their meaning! This is sort of a never-before-known, healthy-concomitant "dependent personality disorder."

St. Augustine in his shortest prayer said it this way,

"Dear God, our hearts are restless until they find their rest in Thee."

God says it this way,

"Dear wonderful recovering Sally and Sam, my heart is restless until it finds its rest in Thee."

(Note: That has to be a classic of anthropomorphism!)

Just two transitive verbs, madly in love with their "direct objects!"

Unfortunately, your "Alcoholic" name tag will always remain. There is an old adage: "all labels are liable." I can guarantee you that you, very much like Hester in The Scarlet Letter, will have to live with your "A" label for the rest of your life. Even in the best of spiritual recoveries from substance abuse, here are a few examples of the type of name difficulty you can expect:

- A Scottish jury, comprised primarily of old fogies, was called in to decide the fate of a body that had been found at the bottom of a well. They had to decide if the victim had fallen or had been pushed. After much deliberation, they came back with the verdict that this was *"An Act Of God, under Highly Suspicious Circumstances!"*

- For centuries, God's refusal to be labeled has driven Orthodox Jews nuts! It's called *the tetragrammaton*, i.e., the nameless name of God. They can't say "It," "Y-H-V-H!" They add, change, and move vowel pointings and come up with variations like Adonoy or Elohim.

- God spelled backwards is . . . Dog! The meaning is not in the word. It is in what we associate with the word, or in what we bring with us when we see or hear it!

- In Aldous Huxley's "Those Barren Leaves," Miss Thriplow was suddenly captivated by the fleeting impulse that she should be more "spiritual." In order to be the most receptive, she "got into bed, and lying on her back, with all her muscles relaxed, she began to think about God." Her imagination started to work:

God is a spirit, she said to herself, a spirit, a spirit. She tried to picture something huge and empty, but alive. A huge flat expanse of sand, for example, and over it a huge blank dome of sky; and above the sand everything should be tremulous and shimmering with heat – an emptiness that was yet alive. A spirit, an all-pervading spirit. God is a spirit. Three camels appeared on the horizon of the sandy plain and went lolloping along in an absurd ungainly fashion from left to right. Miss Thriplow made an effort and dismissed them. God is a spirit, she said aloud. But of all animals camels are really almost the queerest; when one thinks of their frightfully supercilious faces, with their protruding under lips like the last Hapsburg kings of Spain. . . . No, no; God is a spirit, all-pervading, everywhere. All the universes are made one in him.

WORD: THOUGHT IS NOT THE SAME AS AWARENESS!

Alcohol **is** a "false god." To reprise Augustine . . . **your order of loves is changing!**

This is a realization of your heart!

Pause for a moment to feel this new reality. Because of this "love thing" going on with God, alcohol is hardly missed . . . alcohol who?

Your mind agrees!

The exciting answer of recovery is that it is not only a process, **Recovery is Relationship**.

Try to understand. This is a highly contagious disease that you've contracted from being in contact with God. It's the newest exceedingly resistant (modified unselfish) strain of "Dependent Personality Disorder" (Note: Clinically this is impossible! The good news is it doesn't itch and doesn't rot your teeth!) He can't live without you! Despite sounding confusing, this is the healthiest way to start climbing out of the depths of despair. You are not given the option, as in past failed attempts, of reacting to a treatment plan. You are given a relationship!

The fact that we have a word for "God" suggests He is something that can be grasped.

But God is not about to be imprisoned in the identity of a name!

Now, recovery can go one of two ways:

1) Toward: What do you mean?
> What do you mean when I say, what do you mean?
> What do you mean when I say, what do you
> mean, what do you mean?

Or . . .

2) Toward: **"The Singular Love Relationship"** that God intended!

Forget the psychobabble and just think about . . .

The Singular Love Relationship you have in your life.

There is no subject and no object. It's a mutual unfolding! As soon as you try to blurt out how awesome God is as your creator and sustainer and best friend, there is a deep, unexplainable knowing, beautiful beyond belief, that God is saying the same things about <u>you</u>.

Father knows best just doesn't cut it in this relationship!

You can verify this truth with at least a dozen songs that are special to you. Imagine that you are singing them to God and then imagine that God is singing them to you. One of my very special favorites is Neil Diamond's "The Story of My Life":

The story of my life, it's very plain to read,
it starts the day you came
and ends the day you leave.
The story of my life, begins and ends with you
The names are still the same,
The story's still the truth.

that's right . . . allow God to sing that to you!

<u>God cannot be an object without being Subject!</u>

And so we have it . . .

 WORD: This is what you put in place of alcohol:

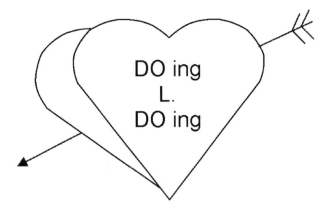

Two hands intertwined, carving two hearts on the old oak tree!

WORD: GOD HAS DONE IT ALL...THE SINGULAR!

"I AM I SAID"

Let's make **"The Singular"** more intelligible:

Remember in Philosophy 101, how you learned about the ancient Greeks and their universal chair? In Hellenism there was only one universal ideal chair. All other chairs were individual entities and not knowable. Individual entities (e.g., a lawn chair, a captain's chair, a folding chair, etc.) could only be thought of as particular instances of a universal. God blows by this with "the singular." To mix the metaphor, your relationship with God is like curling up in your Grandfather's overstuffed Morris chair with the faded blue arm covers. It smelled just like his pipe. Each of us remembers such a chair, and each chair and our experience involving each chair is unique. [Note: We have a really big God on our hands]. Our singular love relationship with God is a lot like this!

Here's a story about God's singular love relationships:

> The preacher one night in church gave an "altar call," and a huge, burly man came storming down the aisle. He was obviously deeply moved and very remorseful. Tears were streaming down his cheeks. He went all the way to the front and said to the preacher:

> "You said that God could save anybody, no matter what they've done, or who they are. I want to believe that. But I want you to know that I've done everything. I've done it all. I have broken every commandment. I've been a terrible sinner and caused great pain to many people. I'm a Swedish blacksmith by trade and I don't know whether God can help me or not."

57

The preacher took the man's massive hand, looked deep into his sad eyes and said:

"Sir, you're in luck. God is specializing in Swedish blacksmiths tonight."

This compassionate story alludes to two critical recovery principles. The first is that recovery is a loving relationship with God and that God actively seeks to establish this relationship. The second, less obvious, principle is that you are no longer alone! This is not a corollary of the first principle. Principal number two shatters the alcoholic's pathological sense of "Terminal Uniqueness." Self-proclaimed stoicism ("If you had my problems, you'd drink too") is dissipated!

Along the same lines, the following "oldie but goodie" puts "Poor, poor, pitiful me; pour me another drink" in its place:

Footprints

One night a man had a dream. He dreamed he was walking along the beach with the Lord. Across the sky flashed scenes from his life. For each scene, he noticed two sets of footprints in the sand: one belonging to him and the other to the Lord.

When the last scene of his life flashed before him, he looked back at the footprints in the sand. He noticed that many times along the path of his life there was only one set of footprints. He also noticed that it happened at the very lowest and saddest times in his life. This really bothered him and he questioned the Lord about it. "Lord, you said that once I decided to follow you, you'd walk with me all the way. But I have noticed that during the most troublesome times in my life, there is only one set of footprints. I don't understand why, when I needed you most, you would leave me."

The Lord replied, "My son, My precious child. I love you
and I would never leave you. During your times of trial and
suffering, when you see only one set of footprints,
it was then that I carried you."

Mary Stevenson

"Footprints" proves to be relevant and timely for many people
in recovery. However, for others, the following authentic story
better explains the nature of this new (or at least newly recognized)
relationship:

A mother, wishing to encourage and inspire her
young son's progress at playing the piano, bought
tickets to a concert of one of the world's greatest
pianists, Ignace Paderewski.

They arrived at the concert hall early, and the
mother began chatting with some friends. The little
boy was fascinated by the grand piano on the stage.
He had never seen such a beautiful instrument. The
mother talked on. She was having a good time catching
up on things, when all of a sudden, the chatter in the
hall abruptly stopped! All eyes turned to the stage
and the little boy, who had slipped away and was
sitting at the piano. He started to play. Everyone in
the auditorium knew the familiar melody: "Twinkle,
twinkle, little star."

The ushers were horrified. The mother was
embarrassed. How could this happen?

An usher dashed toward the stage and was ready to
pluck the boy off the bench, when fate intervened!

Paderewski himself stopped the usher. The great pianist walked up behind the little boy and whispered, "Don't quit. Keep playing."

Then leaning over, Paderewski reached down with his left hand and filled in the bass part. With his right hand he reached around and added accent to the melody! Together the old master and the young novice made beautiful music.

God works like that in our lives!

Don't Quit! Keep Playing!

As you can tell by now, Paul Tillich is one of my favorite theologians. He spoke several times at the College of Wooster in Wooster, Ohio, when I was an undergraduate there. After one of his lectures, the philosophy and religion majors met with him in a question and answer session. Allen S., reflecting the healthy skepticism that seems to pervade the beliefs of many college students, announced to Dr. Tillich, "Dr. Tillich . . . there is no God!" To which Dr. Tillich responded, "Yes, young man, I agree completely . . . now, please be the first to tell me ... what is ... is?"

"The real proof of God is the agonized attempt to deny Him."
(Erich Frank)

The time is right for some **"Religion Bashing"**!

Religion is one of the favorite "dead cats" that people pull out and swing around as a scapegoat for avoiding the need to take a serious look at their drinking or drugging. What they really have a problem with is **"Religiosity"**! I have that same problem!

Dr. Bob Smith, one of the cofounders of AA, also had that same problem. Dr. Bob had been raised in a fanatically rigid Puritanical New England family. "From childhood through high school, I was

60

forced to go to church, Sunday school and evening service [. . .]. This had the effect of making me resolve that when I was free from parental domination, I would never again darken the doors of a church."

The following excerpt from James Fenimore Cooper's "Drums along the Mohawk" is classic stereotypical "New England Puritanism," and, with tongue in cheek, makes our case against "religiosity."

Inside Herkimer Church, "high up, in the shadow of the sounding board," the Reverend Mr. Rozencrantz knelt and prayed:

"*O Almighty God*, we are thinking right now of Mary Marte Wollaber. She is just fifteen years old, but she is going with one of the soldiers at Fort Dayton. He is a Massachusetts man, *O God*, and it has come to my attention that he is married in the town of Hingham. I have had her father and mother talk to her, I have talked to her myself, but she won't pay attention. We ask Thy help, *God Almighty*, in bringing her back to the path of virtue, from which, we believe, she has strayed pretty far.

"*O Almighty God*, You have brought us an early spring, keep off the frosts until the fruit is set. *O Lord*, the English codlin Nicholas Herkimer has grafted onto his Indian apple tree has bloomed this year. May it bear fruit.

[. . .]

"*O Almighty God*, we ask Thy compassion and aid for all of us who are in sickness. We ask it for Petey Paris, who got the flux real bad on Saturday. His Uncle Isaac Paris sent the news up to us and asks our prayers and says that he has got in a new supply of calicos, French reds, broadcloths, [. . .] scythes and grindstones.

[. . .] "*O God Almighty*, our own Colonel Peter Bellinger wants the fourth company to muster at

Dayton tomorrow, June sixteenth. [. . .] May all the militia be punctual to assemble [. . .] at eight o'clock sharp on Monday morning.

"For Christ's sake, Amen."

Religiosity has never been an issue in my life. God has always approached me "in relationship." Here's a real-life analogy. It is my (almost) final aviation story:

My Dad gave me my first airplane ride in 1946, when I was 8 years old. It was in a canvas, open cockpit, single front and back seat, dual control, stick-and-rudder, yellow 1943 Stearman biplane. This was one of the most popular and most loved WWII Trainers. After the war, my father bought 50 of them as surplus. As memory serves me, Dad paid $201.00 for each plane. The cost included having them flown in by WAF's (Women's Air Force), wonderful ladies who would stay at our house overnight and then go back and get more airplanes to "ferry in." Today, if you can even find an air worthy Stearman, the purchase price would be about $150,000!

Dad put me in the front seat. He insisted that I be strapped in and (despite my mother's strong objections) occupy the seat all by myself. I guess it was a nice coincidence that he hopped into the seat behind me. It really wasn't necessary because, he had assured me that I was flying the airplane and I was a great pilot! (Mother: "Now, Maurice James, don't you touch anything!" / Dad: "Now, Mother, he's fine!" He gave one last snug down to the seat belt and added, strangely: "He can't reach!") I was keenly aware of the controls moving. Even the rudder pedals were moving, as if by some mighty, mysterious force. To all appearances, little Maurice James Murray was flying that airplane! I was the front seat "captain."

The privilege of my life has been exactly the same adventure! I still can't reach, but I have my Father / Pilot in the seat behind me, moving the controls!

It reminds me of the line from the beautiful Catholic Hymn "Be Not Afraid."

It has two powerful verses with the refrain:

**"Be not afraid. I go before you always. Come follow me,
and I will give you rest."**

And thus, the apprehensive question ("How Do I Keep From Relapsing?") we opened this chapter with has been replaced with the positive, heartfelt conviction, "I will do everything I can not to betray this "love relationship of my lifetime!"

STOPPING DISTANCES

[Memorize this. It will be an essay question on the Exam.]

[signs point beyond themselves]

"The Paleface" [Starring Bob Hope and Jane Russell]
Directed by Norman Z. McLeod
A Paramount Picture [TCM.com]
1948

Peter "Painless" Potter (Bob Hope) is an incompetent dentist who Calamity Jane, a Federal Agent (Jane Russell) (to fulfill her own clandestine purposes) has tricked into believing is a skilled Indian Fighter. He winds up, dressed in cowboy garb, complete with a six shooter, in the two bit Western Town of "Buffalo Flats" in the "Dirty Shame Saloon" kissing the "Queen of the Saloon" the lovely "Pepper."

This is when things get tense because Pepper is Big Joe's girlfriend and sure enough Big Joe comes storming in and sees the kiss. The two brash warriors go chest to chest and a shoot out challenge at sundown is the result. While waiting for the fateful hour Potter bolsters his courage with many drinks of "Red Eye" at the bar. Finally the fateful time arrives and as Potter staggers toward the swinging doors he gets lots of advice from fellow saloon people:

> "He killed my brother, so here's a tip, he draws
> from the left so lean to the right."
> "Son, I'll let you in on something, long toward
> sunset there's a wind from the East so you better aim
> to the West."

"I know this Joe like a book. He crouches when he shoots so stand on your toes."

As Potter walks down the street toward the gun fight he repeats the tactic's:

"He draws from the left so stand on your toes. There's a wind from the East better lean to the right. He crouches when he shoots, better aim to the West. He draws from his toes so lean toward the wind."

Then he confidently proclaims..."Ah I've got it!"

After a disastrous performance (saved
only by a shot by Calamity Jane)

He rationalizes "The wind shifted!"

So many people are self appointed "Substance Abuse" Counseling Guru's and know how to "fix you" if you simply follow their advice. In The Rooms of AA this is called "taking someone else's inventory."

As memory
serves me
By Mo Murray
Friendly recollections of people, places and events
in the not-too-distant past.

Uncle Doc

Remember when doctors made house calls? Well, I was reminded of it the other day when I came across a cartoon. It depicted an obviously very sick man lying in bed. He was relaying a message to his wife who was nearby holding the telephone. The caption read: "That's all right, dear. Tell the doctor we understand that he no longer makes house calls. If he would be so kind as to have his nurse phone his mailing address to the funeral home, I'll make sure he gets paid – in my will."

In chuckling over that cartoon, I can't help being reminded of our family physician. He not only made house calls, but – believe it or not – he also delivered the milk! Yes, his black bag and his milk bottle tray always sat side by side on the floor boards of his Model A Ford.

We all called him "Uncle Doc." Actually Uncle Doc Beswick was his full name. And I came to know and love him because he spent his summers in a cottage next to ours in the fishing village of South Bowers Beach, Delaware.

As a physician, Uncle Doc Beswick called on many of the cottages. So he thought it prudent and practical – and certainly not beneath his dignity – to also deliver the milk.

I remember it like it was yesterday. Every morning at seven a.m. sharp, I'd hear the "Uga Uga" horn of Uncle Doc's Model A as he backed her out of the metal shed behind his cottage. I'd gobble up the last bite of my soggy cereal and scurry out the door to join him. You know, when it was very hot we'd even push open the front windshield to get the breeze.

I guess it's no wonder that some of the tourists were skeptical about Uncle Doc. Especially when he appeared at the steps lugging his black case in one hand and the gray metal basket of milk bottles in the other. But those of us who had stepped on a rusty nail or suffered near sun stroke knew what a medical wonder he was.

Uncle Doc's been gone over 25 years now. And during my last summer vacation back home, my Mother recalled that I had only been to his office once – the time he removed some dog bite stitches from my left leg.

Recalling that visit made my Mother and I decide to get into the car and hurry down to Uncle Doc's old office. I was as excited as I've ever been. You see, Uncle Doc Beswick's office was up some side wooden steps over an old hardware story just off the main drag. When we got there, we found that the store was vacant and those time-worn steps had been removed. But we did find what we really came for. What my Mother and I had both recalled was a wooden, hand-painted sign nailed at the front of the steps to Uncle Doc's office. Sure enough, it was still there. And we both agreed that it made a fitting epitaph for a man whom we felt sure the good Lord had rewarded for caring so much about people.

As memory serves me, the faded sign very simple read: "Doc Beswick – upstairs."

6

Swat that bee on your recovery door knob!

ASSIGNMENT #4:

"MO'S Map and the San Francisco Cable Car"

This assignment title is not my ego gone mad. It conveys, as an acronym, what has been the essential message that Finnegan has been singing to you all along, with an added emphasis on "Recovery as a process." Finnegan sings "Begin again," and **MOS** implores you to persevere with "**M**ore **O**f **S**ame." More daily positive actions! Use : **MAP: M**o's **A**ction **P**lan!

 **WORD: THE WAY IT IS**

a) You are pulling the process of your recovery into your newly rediscovered love relationship with God!

b) You are not pushing your newly rediscovered relationship with God into your recovery process!

Recovery requires conscious, continuous, positive actions.

There is no such thing as no action. A decision not to decide is a decision. Unconscious behaviors tend to sabotage recovery. The status quo is more comfortable and less frightening than the new unknown.

What follows in the next few pages are some rote, mechanical things to do. They will help get rid of "unconstructive suffering" and replace it with "constructive suffering." I'm sorry there is no "easier, softer way!"

These were left until last so the essence of relationship recovery could be established!

YOUR ASSIGNMENT:

ALWAYS HAVE A PENCIL HANDY!

IF I EVER CATCH YOU WITHOUT A PENCIL,
YOUR GRADE FOR THE ENTIRE WORKBOOK WILL BE
AN "F"
A pencil is that important!
Positive recovery thoughts are like *slippery fish*!
You can drop them overboard in an instant!
In fact, not having a pencil is a major cause of relapse!

Here's what happens. It's called: **"Maximizing and Minimizing!"** It works like this. The longer you remain in sobriety the more you tend to take the advantages of sober life for granted and start to **minimize** them. Sobriety becomes boring! During that same time you tend to forget the miseries associated with your drinking days and start to **maximize** your "good old drinking days! **Stinking Thinking** restarts its whisper, "there were some good times, all I have to do is stop in time." Here's how they state this principle in the rooms of AA:

Write this down ...

"The farther away you are from your last drink, the closer you are to your next drink!"

Now here's a "Cable Car" formula coming up:

Write it down!

HEAD ↔ HEART ↔ BEHAVIOR = RELATIONSHIP RECOVERY
WITH GOD!

As a cable car "gripman" of your own "POWELL & HYDE Sts." Car, you will become an expert on. . .

     1) How to run your brain
     2) How to run your heart.

     which informs you . . .

     3) How to run your behaviors.

The three blend together in this cliché from AA rooms:

"Healthy thinking can't lead to Sober living. But Sober living can lead to healthy thinking!"
The formula will become automatic.
For now, write it down!

The San Francisco Cable Car analogy is the most appropriate and limitless one imaginable for this situation. Here's what you need to know:

You are the gripman on your own "POWELL & HYDE Sts." car. (Note: try to get car number 505, 515, or 518). As gripman, you pull the grip lever, track brake lever, emergency brake lever, and step on the wheel brake pedal. The "grip" is a mechanism that grasps the cable and makes you go.

You are the gripman on your own "POWELL & HYDE Sts." car, instead of on a California Street car ("Van Ness Ave, California & Market Streets"), for several reasons.

First, the California Street car goes only straight up and down the same street. There are no curves! Your car encounters sharp curves! Both routes often drop down into foggy spots in the valley and have long climbs up steep grades before starting to race downward, where every gripman must obey the large "sign" painted on the pavement to **"LET GO"** and release the cable immediately! Sometimes, after the cable has been dropped, the car must coast on its momentum past a danger point. All gripmen then have to wait for another large sign painted on the pavement that reads **"TAKE ROPE."**

Second, the California cars are five feet longer, which allows them to have controls at both ends. The gripman is completely independent and simply takes a short walk to change directions. As gripman on your Powell Street car, you have to deal with "turntables." **Turning the car is not a one-man job. You need help! Helpful people ("Support") will come from everywhere!** The double clang of the bell, by the conductor, indicating that you are once again rolling in the desired direction, makes all the effort worth it!

Finally, Powell cars are Irish green . . . for **go!** California cars are red. Need I say more?

Traveling down the 18" drop from the head to the heart goes like this:

When you think this . . . what do you feel?
When you feel that . . . what do you want to do?

Traveling up the 18" incline from the heart to the head goes like this:

When you feel this . . . what do you think?
When you think that . . . what do you want to do?

The curves, slopes, grades, fog, traffic jams, and other factors make unconscious decisions a set-up for a relapse collision! One of the most commonly arrived at "bottom line" answers that you can take with you to the "car barn" at the end of each day is:

There is no situation so bad that a drink or a drug won't make it worse!

You'll remember the emphasis by Ben Hogan on the importance of details when he was dealing with mechanical aspects of the golf swing. It's equally important to remember that his overview of "playing the game of golf" emphasized **VFR:**

Visualize - ing

Feel - ing

Rhythm

Visualizing (Head): Job had a lot of problems. My father, when I was at the height of my addiction, once said to me, "Son, you are my Job!" For you and me and Job, recovery was assured when we saw God!

For Job, "awareness" is the definition of God:

"I have heard of thee by the hearing of
the ear: but now mine eye seeth thee."
(Job 42:5)

Feeling (Heart): In the rooms of AA they say, "you have to feel it to heal it!"

Rhythm (Behavior/Life): This is "the dance of love" you'll experience with God. It's real and fun and you'll want to have your drapes closed when you start dancing around so nobody dials 911 and has you shipped off to "the funny farm!"

"SMOKER": The heartache lies not in the beverage but in a person's life!

Some of you may remember the childhood fable "The Nightingale and The Peddler."

As the story goes, the Nightingale didn't want to go through the daily chore of digging up enough worms to eat, so she met the peddler along the side of the roadway every day and exchanged one feather for one worm. It was a painless type of daily transaction, and I can remember that, even at an early age, I was able to predict the outcome. Pretty soon the little Nightingale had traded so many feathers to the Peddler, it couldn't fly anymore!

But until recently, I had forgotten the real tragic part of that story:

One anxious morning, the Nightingale approached the Peddler and wanted to reverse the trade. The Peddler answered bluntly:

"My business is worms for feathers . . . not feathers for worms!"

It's been said that there are only two types of pain in life:

1) **The pain of discipline and**
2) **The pain of regret**

PUT THAT IN YOUR PIPE AND SMOKE IT!

It's taken awhile, but everything that has gone before has been absolutely necessary. You had to have something to fill that big hole in the center of your existence! Think back to the multiple-choice question.

Faith is not a will to believe.
Recovery is not a will to stop drinking.

There is no faith, there is no recovery, without a content toward which it is directed! After the acknowledged death of Ethyl, if you were left to unconscious forces in your recovery, compulsions would creep in and set you up to relapse! You had to be introduced to **a loving relationship with God "as you understand him"** (AA / The Big Book).

Otherwise, here are some examples of the potentially disastrous scenarios you could be encountering:

A man was driving at night somewhere in the upper Midwest, in the middle of a blinding snowstorm. He was about to take his chances, pull off the roadway, and wait it out, when, as if a gift sent from heaven, there appeared right in front of him a snow plow! The man was elated and felt reassured that by following the snowplow he would eventually reach a safe haven. The pace was slow, but he was dedicated to his plan and gripped the steering wheel with stoic determination. Time passed. More time passed. He remained a resolute "follower." Finally, after several hours, the snowplow stopped and the driver got out and walked back to the man's car. The man rolled the window down and was greeted with these words:

"Sir, I don't know where you're going, but I thought it only fair
to tell you that I'm almost finished plowing this lot."

In a similar way, I can vividly remember, years ago, when my mediocre do-it-yourself home repair skills failed me. I had been trying to fix a leak under the kitchen sink. After an hour or so, I finally surrendered and called in a plumber. The plumber fixed the leak very quickly, and when my daughter asked him what had been the problem, he answered, "Your father got hold of some tools."

You want things to go in the opposite direction...

A farmer needed a helper, so he posted a notice in the village. Three promising young men responded, and the farmer met with each one of them in turn. He asked the first about his background and then concluded the interview with a peculiar question:

"Tell me, how long can you work with a stone in your shoe?"

Without hesitation the answer came:
"Half a day."

The farmer thanked him and proceeded to talk to the second young man, once again concluding with the question:
"How long can you work with a stone in your shoe?"

This young man boasted:
"All day long."

The farmer sent him on his way and then interviewed the third youth. Once again he asked the peculiar question:
"How long can you work with a stone in your shoe?"

This youth exclaimed:
"Not one minute. When I get a stone in my shoe, I take it out right away."

The farmer hired the third young man on the spot.
I call this the "aim, aim, aim, aim, syndrome."

Now use your skills . . . and fire!

Look at the essential skills you already have and almost forgot ("slippery fish") until now.

I wrote these down for you . . .

Acknowledgements:

1. You can't change what you don't acknowledge. Done
2. I drank to escape from some reality I didn't want to face. Done
3. I drank to escape "nothingness." Now it's God and me! Done
4. I drank for short term pleasure, which led to long term pain. Done
5. Alcohol served a purpose; it didn't meet a need. Done
6. I didn't get in trouble every time I drank, but whenever I got in trouble, I had been drinking. Done
7. There is no situation so bad that a drink won't make it worse! Done
8. Misuse / Overuse / "White Knuckle Sobriety" / Escape / Crutch Cravings / "I must have a drink or I'll die!" Done
9. I'm ready to "get real" with myself. Done

I'm the only deal I have and now I can present myself even up with God and the world!

Lest you forget, here comes that classic recovery advice:

"EASY DOES IT!"

Allow yourself to start slow and walk on the shady side of the street.

Rediscover a love of silence!

Silence **is** golden!

Cut out the quadraphonic, fully modulated **noise** . . . CNN . . . MTV . . . CD'S . . . DVD'S . . . the in-your-house, in-your-car **noise**.

 **WORD: Listening vs. Noise**

In the earliest days of AA, back in Akron, Ohio, in the late 1930's, all new members were not allowed to talk ("share") for their first year when attending meetings. The old adage can still be heard in AA rooms today: "You have two ears and one mouth, so listen twice as much as you speak!"

This is especially important in your newly reestablished relationship with God. If, as the Bible declares, God is the "still small voice" that speaks to you out of "the whirlwind and fire," you'll have to listen for that voice very carefully!

Imagine if I had this long distance phone conversation with my daughter in California:

"Hi, honey, it's your old dad. I love you! I sure hope everything is all right out there. It looks like you're getting some rain. I have a tee time in 35 minutes so I don't have much time. I sure hope I hit my driver as well as I've been hitting it on the range. I love you so much! Got to run, so I'll let you go!" . . . "It's sure nice talking to you" ("Cat's in the Cradle," Harry Chapin).

So . . . cut out the noise of being a human echo, even on your cell phone . . .

let it go!

One of the benefits of listening is that you are more alert. This is important because a relapse just doesn't happen! There are warning signs **("LET GO," "GRAB ROPE")** that, if ignored, lead to triggers. Just as successful recovery leaves clues, relapse also leaves clues in advance of the event. In AA they call these "dry drunk" behaviors "Bud," "Building up to drink." By the time you get to a trigger, it is probably already too late. The expression is, "your elbow is already bent!" The comparison is often made, again, to a man jumping, this time off a cliff. A lot of noticeable, increasingly perilous things occur as he walks up to the edge! But you must be paying attention!

Here are the four most common warning signs:

I've painted them in big letters on the pavement in front of you . . .

"HALT"
Never allow yourself to get too. . .

1) H ungry
2) A ngry
3) L onely
4) T ired

Next . . .

Write this in your "gripman training manual". . .

DON'T "SHOULD" ON YOURSELF TODAY!

Do your best to take the mandates (the "should's" and the "must's") out of your life, as well as the injunctions (the "should not's" and "must not's")

When you direct a "should/must" toward another person ("He should do this."), it leads to a resentment and, if unheeded, to anger and rage. When you point the finger of a "should" or a "must" toward yourself, it leads to shame and, if left to fester, to guilt.

There are many appropriate emotions, such as anger. Rage, however, is inappropriate. Sadness is a normal human response.

Despair and depression aren't. **Don't "should" on yourself or others, and you'll come to know a new daily emotional balance!**

This one conscious effort on your part will work miracles . . . and lead you toward this familiar prayer:

The Serenity Prayer

God, grant me the Serenity
To accept the things I cannot change,
Courage to change the things I can,
And the Wisdom to know the difference.
Amen.

Reinhold Neibuhr

 **GROW UP OR THROW UP:**

Mo throws up on "The Serenity Prayer!"

I have to tell this story on myself. Among other things, it illustrates the tendency I had during my first few AA meetings to "qualify myself out" ("I'm not like these coffee-guzzling, chain-smoking strangers; I hadn't yet heard, "we get them from Yale or jail"). And it reflects my "terminal uniqueness" (nobody except me is smart enough or sympathetic enough to understand or care about me except me). Most obviously it reveals how much of an "arrogant ass" I was.

The first childish thing about these people was the way they hung those immature signs all over the walls:

FIRST THINGS FIRST / EASY DOES IT / LET GO AND LET
GOD / THIS TOO WILL PASS / ONE DAY AT A TIME / IT CAN
BE DONE / THINK THINK THINK / FEEL IT TO HEAL IT

But the worst of the lot was that kindergarten, Dr. Suess-sounding "Serenity Prayer". It really made me want to throw up! Then one day I learned ("Ah-Ha"): Reinhold Neibuhr wrote "The Serenity Prayer." My "Reiny!" My all-time favorite theologian! My Reiny, who wrote, along with over 500 other books and articles, "The Nature and Destiny of Man," a definitive study of over 600 pages. My "Reiny," from whom I was able to take a few seminars at Union Theological Seminary in New York City shortly before he died. My "Reiny," whom I had impetuously hugged when I first had a chance to meet him, in one of those dim granite Union Seminary hallways! What a memory! Needless to say, my view of those simplistic prescriptions for living began to change!

As I got more days of sobriety, the pithy, catchy little signs began to take on meaning for me. They, as all good signs do, began to point beyond themselves. I could begin to understand how they had become "tried and true" recovery tools. Yes, they were simple, catchy platitudes, but they were also easily-recalled (in times of need) **guides for action!**

Here's another great prescription for your daily well being:

YESTERDAY, TODAY AND TOMORROW

There are two days in every week about which we
should not worry, two days which should be kept free
from fear and apprehension.

One of these days is yesterday, with its mistakes and cares,
its faults and blunders, its aches and pains.
Yesterday has passed forever beyond our control.

All the money in the world cannot bring back yesterday.
We cannot undo a single act we performed. We cannot erase
a single word we said. Yesterday is gone.

The other day we should not worry about is tomorrow,

with its possible adversities, its burdens, its large
promise, and poor performance. Tomorrow is also
beyond our immediate control. Tomorrow's sun will
rise, either in splendor or behind a mask of clouds, but
it will rise. Until it does, we have no stake in tomorrow,
for it is yet to be born.

This leaves only one day – today. Any person can fight the
battles of just one day. It is only when you and I add
the burden of those two awful eternities, yesterday
and tomorrow, that we break down. It is not the
experience of today that drives us mad. It is the
remorse or bitterness of something which happened
yesterday and the dread of what tomorrow may bring.
Let us therefore live but one day at a time.

Anonymous

Jesus put it in fewer words:

"Take therefore no thought for the morrow:
for the morrow shall take thought for the
things of itself. Sufficient unto the day is the evil thereof."
(Matthew 6:34)

The "Good News" is … you are "in recovery" now!

These are the same words that opened this Driver's Manual, only now you cannot get the singing voice of God out of your head:

"The story of my life, it's very plain to read,
it starts the day you came
and ends the day you leave."

Here is my last aviation story. I soloed in 1958 in a stick-and-rudder Aeronca Tri-Champ. Two years later I got my "single engine land" license in the same "bird." I can vividly remember my strong emotional response as I got out of the airplane after my first flight. I never wanted my instructor to ever leave me alone in that cockpit. Twenty training flight hours later, I couldn't wait for him to get <u>out!</u>

This next story reflects the same emotional learning curve:

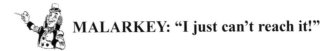 **MALARKEY: "I just can't reach it!"**

A man was retelling a childhood adventure of being chased across a field by a mad bull. The only chance he had to escape was to run fast enough to reach a lone oak tree in the middle of the field. If his little legs could achieve that goal, he then faced the next problem of being able to jump high enough to grab on to the first limb and reach safety.

He paused in the recounting and everyone could tell he was reliving the emotional event. His head started to shake back and forth in a negative way. He again began to speak in a slow, discouraged tone,

"I felt sure that I could reach the tree before the bull, but I also knew **I could never jump high enough to reach that branch!**" He stopped again as if not wanting his listeners to hear the worst.

The suspense was too much to bear: "Well, did you catch the branch?"

"No, I missed it," he broke out in a big smile,

"but I caught it on the way down!"
And with that same display of confidence in your abilities,

It's time for me to get out of this airplane before you shove me
out!

You can do it!
God bless you, and enjoy your recovery!
Mo

STOPPING DISTANCES

[signs point beyond themselves]

Your Mother always told you
"Don't play with matches!"

- Don't Romance the Drink
- Stop lounging in your drinking habit
- Give up your "Alcoholic Fun Drunk" Aura

If you don't then "the expectation of craving" will become the threshold of a problem with alcohol.

Craving is to a large extent, especially with alcohol, a result of learning.

G. Alan Marcatt, a leading researcher in adolescent alcohol drinking, conducted a clinical study in a Bar with College Students. It was described to the participants as being a standard fifty/fifty study. However, Marcatt didn't play by the rules. All the drinks that were served were "placebo." Guess what. Within fifteen minutes the entire "test group" had "the placebo" effect and was "acting out" as if they were on an "Alcohol Fun Drunk."

The point is that it became, not the beverage, but "the craving" for the effect of being drunk that was most important.

As memory serves me
By Mo Murray
Friendly recollections of people, places and events
in the not-too-distant past.

Haunted House

When you were a kid, was there a haunted house in your home town? If there was, you were really lucky. I mean all you had to do late at night was walk by that haunted house. And you probably breathed a sigh of relief that you didn't have to go in.

Well, I had the bone-chilling privilege of actually living in the haunted house of Dover, Delaware. Not only that, my study room was where the resident ghost of an old Revolutionary War General used to appear most often.

The name of our home was "Woodburn." It was built in the early seventeen hundreds with bricks brought over as ballast on the ships from England. And let me tell you, Woodburn had all the necessary elements for a triple A approved haunted house. There were secret passageways in the basement that, before the Civil War, were part of the infamous Underground Railroad. And that's where hundreds of fleeing slaves had died. The giant tulip-poplar tree in the yard was hollowed out and carried the legend of being the town hanging tree. There were even secret compartments and an escape tunnel that went back to Jones Creek and that led – now get this – into Murderkill River. How's that for a blood curdling name!

But back during the Revolution, Woodburn served as a hospital. That's when the General I was telling you about died there. I guess he just liked the place so much he decided to take up permanent residence.

Now, folks, believe me . . . it's all true! In fact, the Reverend Lorenzo Dow, who was a prominent Methodist minister of yesteryear, talks in one of his books about being a house guest at Woodburn. He recalls asking the family to wait before having him offer the prayer at breakfast. You see, he wanted the friendly old gentlemen he had passed on the steps to join them. You guessed it. That was the General. Probably out taking his early morning stroll.

In more violent times, Patty Cannon, who was a notorious slave trader, raided the house to get some more merchandise to sell down South. History tells us that one time things go so bad for poor Patty that she sold her own grandmother. Which only proves that blood isn't always thicker than money.

But these days I have to feel sorry for the ghost of the old General. You see, now this noble spirit is busy spooking Woodburn's six-hundred thousand new owners.

You see, my Dad sold our great haunted house to the State of Delaware for a Governor's mansion. So, technically, Woodburn is now owned by all six-hundred thousand citizens of that State. And every Tuesday and Thursday afternoon they stomp through its haunted halls hunting for the General.

But as memory serves me, my ghostly friend is probably hiding back in my study, still laboring over the last Algebra problem he was helping me with. Don't laugh . . . ghosts are good at Algebra. Why, without his help I would never have passed the course.

7

Now I lay me down to … marinate!

This is the most important and powerful activity of your Recovery. Nightly, at bedtime, you will reaffirm your Recovery by starting with the simple words of your childhood prayer. "Now I lay me down to (and here comes the new part) affirm that alcohol is no longer in control of my life!"

The preceding one hundred pages have been a prelude to this simple, life changing "bedtime" ritual. Feel free to put the mantra in your own words so that it captures your emotional self.

Here again are the very first words that you read when you opened the front cover of this book. It's "The Corner Stone" of your Recovery and like all great insight, it's very easy to understand:

The Greatest Discovery

The greatest discovery of the 19th century was not in the realm of physical sciences, but the power of the subconscious mind touched by faith. Any individual can tap into an eternal reservoir of power that will enable them to overcome any problem that may arise. All weaknesses can be overcome.

William James
Harvard Psychologist
The Father of American Psychology

Every subsequent word of text was motivated by this quotation and was focused on leading you back to a safe, sober and happy life.

From page one I've been working on making the "Reality of Your Recovery" **your most dominant thought**. Eastern Wisdom emphasizes, that from birth until death we constantly move in the direction of our most dominant thought. Positive daily behavioral modifications are important, but they are not as "free standing" as they might appear to be. They are in fact initiated by the power of your subconscious mind. The positive input of your subconscious mind is the grappling hook that maintains the reality of your life and your recovery.

You don't need a hypnotherapist. "Stare into my eyes" said Dr. Potato Head, the hypnotist. All you need to do is truly understand the functioning power of the subconscious mind. In overcoming an addiction to alcoholism we are dealing with "Behavior Modification" and in Behavior Modification "depth of trance" plays only a minor role or no roll at all.

It's imperative that we debunk hypnosis as a "self help gimmick."

Your subconscious mind is "The Motor" of your recovery. Messier Mesmer with all his bells, whistles, animal magnetism, candles and spiral hypno discs couldn't hypnotize you out of your own shadow. His problem, in recovery terms, would be your denial and in clinical terms would be your resistance.

Q: How many hypnotists does it take to change a light bulb?
A: Only One. But the light bulb must want to change.

Let's review the "golden" or "magical" simple exercise, the life changer.

- OUT WITH THE OLD ("the old" had you trapped):

Kicking "Shouda' Coulda' Woulda' to the curb."

Every night, just before sleep (half in & half out) which is actually a very receptive trance state; you start with your new recovery affirmation. It's important for you to know that **you are already who you think you are**. In these nightly five minutes you are creating a new and greater value of yourself!

Your subconscious mind is impartial. It doesn't reason why. If you FEEL IT… if you KNOW IT… your subconscious mind will BUY IT! You **FEEL the truth** when you say: **"I am in Recovery Now!"**

You kick out your old "self speak" i.e. "I can't do this. I can't overcome my drinking. I'm sick! I don't deserve any better!"

I call this the "I Suck" Syndrome.

It's actually easy to pivot this around with your new recovery skills. It's called… "Correcting Backwards." The tag phrase is "Best Lessons are Learned Lessons."

This nightly moment in time is <u>not</u> about WHAT YOU WANT. It is about:

WHO YOU ARE!

 **SMOKER:**

A Psychoanalytic Purist's will recognize this as a core symptom of Freud's "Seduction Theory of Neurosis." You are dealing here with displacing deeply rooted, fundamental "adaptive forces" imbedded within your now antiquated addictive personality." Wow! **Put That in Your Pipe and Smoke It!**

- IN WITH THE NEW:

You're going to replace your "Worry Time" self-confirming bias with a new mental marinate of Positive Affirmations.

You are already who you think you are. You are already on the other side of addiction. Every night just before nodding off you proclaim your new condition to your subconscious mind.

Steven Covey in his book "The 7 Habits of Highly Effective People" [Simon & Schuster, New York, NY Edition 2001] alludes to this in Habit #2 "begin with the end in mind." However, as you nestle in, preparing for sleep, what you are doing is so very much more. You are in fact already living from the end. You <u>FEEL</u> the truth when you say:

I am in Recovery Now!

Remember, no behavior is ever removed without another taking its place.

If you want to accomplish something you must expect it of yourself.

 **GROW UP OR THROW UP:**

Does this sound sickeningly familiar: "I am good enough, I am smart enough...and daw gone it I'm worth it." Right...Daily Affirmation with Stuart Smalley Al Franken.

- Remember... this is not about what you want; it's about **who you are!** This is an action, not a wish. A wish is a fantasy and is passive. It's not a want. The "action prayer" may be labeled as an "obsessive compulsive ritual" but I view it as a persistent, specific will to action! This is not a Stuart Smalley collection of useful aphorisms assembled into a ritualistic mantra.

- Remember... your subconscious mind is **impartial. It doesn't reason why.** If you **feel** it, your subconscious mind will "**buy it.**"

- These sleepy time sessions are "retraining" your subconscious mind.

An Easy Self-Hypnosis Induction:

There are hundreds of positive useful "self-hypnosis" inductions, just "Google It." This one will tuck in nicely after the opening line of your nightly prayer:

⇒ **SEE... The positive images you have gotten from this book...**

You have the recovery skills and you have...
"your existing recovery drive state."
Self-Hypnosis is internalizing these skills... now!

Note: Our conscious mind is the gatekeeper of all information submitted to the subconscious mind. See if this doesn't sound familiar:

Mo's Conscious Mind Gatekeeper to Mo's Subconscious Mind:

"Mo's going to try to tell you to make those 9th Step Amends again. Those people don't want to hear his old 'I'm Sorry' line one more time."

Mo's Conscious Mind Gatekeeper:

I can't get sober... I need help... hey!
I can't stay sober... I need help... hey!

Will power has nothing to do with it!

With these recovery drive skills, will power is the answer to a question you didn't even ask.

5,283 sheep were exported from Ecuador in 1938.
[Funk and Wagnalls]

That's a ridiculous answer because you didn't ask the question.

Will power is an emotion and as an emotion it comes and goes. Your new recovery skills and existing recovery drive state are here for the duration.

⇒ **HEAR...Shout it from the house tops...**

You have the recovery skills and you have...
"your existing recovery drive state!"
Self-Hypnosis is internalizing these skills... <u>now</u>!

In order to get a sense for what's going on here, let's make a very simplified comparison of the functioning purpose of the conscious mind to the functioning purpose of the subconscious mind:

- The Conscious Mind: looks, listens and learns. It reasons and judges. It analyzes and criticizes. It can accept or reject.
- The Subconscious Mind: runs all bodily functions (e.g. breathing: inhale / exhale). It harbors all images, ideas or concepts (everything you have ever seen, felt, heard, tasted or touched is registered there). **It can and must <u>act out</u> the image, will or concept that you implant into it!**

$\Rightarrow$ **FEEL... you know in your heart of hearts...**

You have the recovery skills and you have...
"your existing recovery drive state!"
Self-Hypnosis is internalizing these skills... <u>now</u>!

The Subconscious Mind is an actor. It must act out!

Good Job! You have just learned to "Trust Yourself!"

 **SMOKER:**

What skills? Don't you dare make a list [too many books on self-hypnosis suggest this]. You don't want to "reactivate" the conscious mind. In your best meditative mode go through the SEE HEAR FEEL sequence three times with your own input, then two, then one. Clinically speaking this "depotentiates" the conscious mind. More simply it "bypasses the capacity of the conscious mind." Finally, our "Now I lay me down to... marinate" technique preempts the self-hypnosis books that warn you not lie on your back because you might fall asleep. It is a proven psychological fact that the very last image, idea or concept repeated to you, by you or through you as you lose consciousness will continually be repeated within the subconscious "acting" mind all night long.

Your Recovery is not a dream!

Enjoy It!

8

A funny thing happened on my way to Recovery!

If I had been capable of writing this book in Hebrew (my 50 year old Seminary Hebrew 101 is a bit rusty) it would have been immediately funny to you because you would have to read the jokes from right to left. Also you would have opened "CAR" and started here at this last chapter, first.

Recovery does start with a revival of your sense of humor.

This disease is serious but we don't have to be. Keep reading and you'll see what I mean:

Only to another drunk can you make the most horrible admissions and make that person laugh.

It gets better…
Then it gets worse…
Then it gets real…
Then it gets different…
Then it gets real different…

A reason to be grateful for your recovery: You wake up instead of coming to.

Definition of an alcoholic: Someone you don't like who drinks as much as you do.

My disease does a marvelous imitation of clarity.

Alcohol allowed me to act irresponsibly and irrationally with great confidence.

Alcoholic Sick -Humor:

I was like a bank; you'd better get to me before 3 P.M.

I was a periodic drinker. I drank period.

If the back of your head keeps getting hit by the toilet seat, you may be an alcoholic.

I'll have what the guy on the floor is having.

One tequila, two tequila, three tequila… floor.

I didn't have a drinking problem, I had a stopping problem.

United we stand, divide we stagger.

Show me a crisis and I'll show you a happy alcoholic.

When you're in a dispute, remember it takes forty muscles to frown but only four to extend your right arm and smack them.

For an alcoholic something is wrong, when nothing is wrong.

Alcoholics don't have relationships, they take hostages.

Why do all alcoholics have arthritis? They are always stiff in one joint or another.

> If a fly lands in the beer of a normal drinker,
> He will order a new beer.
> If a fly lands in the beer of a problem drinker,
> He will wave it away and drink the beer.
> If a fly lands in the beer of an alcoholic,
> He will pick it up by its wings, shake it and shout,
> "Spit it out, spit it out!"

Me-Humor:

I started getting better when I got out of the Self Help Section.

The problem with all these self-help books is that there has to be a self there to help.

I keep trying to make myself a "finished product."

By loving myself, I'm in the perfect relationship.

No one has more humility than me.

Don't try to be a saint before next Thursday.
Bill W

I'm really a very persuasive person; I can convince myself of anything.

When I'm in my head, I start to believe my own press releases.

Why is it I'm most effective when I'm deceiving myself?

I could always make things happen, I just couldn't make them work.

People in recovery can be very opinionated and often wrong, but never in doubt.

I didn't think I was judgmental, I thought I was right.

The only way to get to be right is to give up being right.

Some of us, before we started our recovery, participated in a reign of error.

I have a new philosophy; I'm only going to dread one day at a time.
Charles M. Schultz

I try to take one day at a time but lately several days have attacked me all at once.

I have a lot better problems today than I've ever had.

Your sole purpose in life may be simply to serve as a warning to others.

It's the things I do wrong, my failings that are often the bridge to other people.

Some days you're the pigeon and some days you're the statue.

Stinkin' Thinkin'- Humor:

If alcohol is the answer to your problem, what's the question?

Sometimes I have some questions about the way I think.

Of all the things I lost as a result of my alcoholism, I miss my mind the most.

I know I'm having a bad day when my mind keeps arguing with myself and I don't know which side to take.

Three words you don't want to hear an alcoholic say, "I've been thinking."

Don't believe everything you think.

I'm on the other side of something, but I don't know what it is yet.

I knew so much more than I understood.

Thank you for all the good I did today and all the good I did by not doing.

Becoming aware of my character defects leads me to the next step… blaming my parents.

I came from a normal family, both my parents were dysfunctional.

"This is easy" translates into getting by, but not going through.

The best way out is almost always through.

It is in the going through that the wisdom emerges.

The road to success is always under construction.

If you're not happy today, what day are you waiting for?

If you can't be happy with what you have, how can you be happy with more?

God-Humor:

I am my own higher power.

God help me to be the person my dog thinks that I am.

There are two kinds of people: Those who say to God "Thy will be done" and those to whom God says "All right then, have it your way."

C.S. Lewis

Believe in God, it's easier than coming up with bail money.

Most people want to serve God, but only in an advisory capacity.

God helps those who don't try to take over His work.

If you no longer feel close to God, who moved?

The Church is near but the road is icy.
The Bar is far away but I'll walk carefully.

In tough situations alcoholics tend to use the foxhole prayer: "O God if you will just get me out of this one…"

If you pray and don't get what you ask for, it doesn't mean that your prayer wasn't answered; it means the answer is "No."

Lead me not into temptation. I can find it myself.

My spiritual awakening occurred when there was a flash of light with a cop behind it.

We all know that God never closes one door without opening another, but it can be very scary and painful in that long dark hallway.

I know God doesn't give me anything that I can't handle. I just wish He didn't have such a high opinion of me.

AA and Step-Humor:

This is a suggested program. A judge suggested that I come.

Try AA for 90 days. If you are not totally satisfied we will gladly refund your misery.

Overheard in an AA meeting, "Our leaders are but twisted servants."

Happiness is opening the refrigerator door and seeing your sponsor's face on the side of a milk carton.

The still resentful Alcoholics 8th Step: "Make a list of all people we have harmed and ask God to remove them all."

God grant me the courage to change the things I can't accept.

What keeps AA alive are pilgrims not evangelist.

Fix Others-Humor:

Alcoholics have their arms wrapped around the bottle and Codependents have their arms wrapped around the alcoholic.

Having a tremendous capacity for alcohol may make us proud, but it's like telling someone who has tuberculosis that they cough very well.

Having a relationship in early recovery is like putting "Miracle-Gro" on your "character defects."

Some people will never get ulcers. They're just carriers.

When I go to an AA meeting, I come in with a list of people who need to be there.

Nothing so needs reforming as other people's habits.

Mark Twain

Don't try to make pigs sing. It's a waste of time and it annoys the pigs.

Mark Twain

I don't approach life as a problem to be solved. I approach life as a problem to be avoided.

I'm a professional balker. I'm very afraid of change. I'm the type of person that if I fall into a rut, I'll start hanging pictures, move in and make it a home.

Serenity Sam

More Philosophy Than-Humor:

We didn't get here by eating too much ice cream.

You're only as sick as your secrets.

Believe those who are seeking the truth; doubt those who have found it.

André Gide

When you drink you lose the right to be right.

A fanatic is one who can't change his mind and won't change the subject.

Winston Churchill

Even when you're on the right track, you'll get run over if you just sit there.

Will Rogers

When you do all the talking you only learn what you already know.

The toughest lesson to learn is probably the one you thought you already learned.

Neurosis is the avoidance of experiencing legitimate pain.

Carl Jung

We don't see the world as it is. We see the world as we are.

There is no right or wrong there are only consequences.

Alcohol is a solvent. It will remove everything from your life.

There is no chemical solution to a spiritual problem.

After all is said and done, more is said than done.

It's better to be silent and thought a fool than to open your mouth and remove all doubt.

Will Rogers

Give up the hope of a better past.

There is no right way to do the wrong thing.

The truth shall set you free, but first it will hurt like hell.

Think for yourself, and let others enjoy the privilege of doing so too.

Voltaire

If you don't like what people are saying about you, maybe you should stop doing the things they are talking about.

Best If Used Before/Dated-Humor:

None of us came here on a winning streak.

Alcoholism is an equal opportunity destroyer.

We suffer from alcohol-ism not alcohol-was-ism.

One thing you don't hear when you get sober is "Keep It Complicated."

A bend in the road is not the end of the road, unless you fail to make the turn.

We're lost, but we're making good time.

In my life I was either swinging or ducking.

Relax. Easy Does It. No good alcoholic has to worry about his addiction disappearing overnight.

And finally ...

Please God, teach me to laugh again...
But don't let me ever forget that I cried!

Easy does it!

Mo

APPENDIX

In addition to the sheet music for "Michael Finnegan," I have reprinted four "words of wisdom" from the text. They are among my personal favorites. I made them "clipable," and I hope that with a few handy dandy "pizza" magnets you will add them to your "Fridge Philosophy Collection."

"Finnegan Begin Again"

There was an old man named Mich - ael Fin - negan

He grew whis - kers on his chin again

He Shaved them off but they grew back in again

Poor old Michael Finnegan begin again!

Attitude

The longer I live, the more I realize the impact of attitude
on life. Attitude, to me, is more important than facts. It
is more important than the past, than education, than
money, than circumstances, than failures, than successes,
than what other people think or say or do. It is more
important than appearance, giftedness or skill. It will
make or break a company . . . a church . . . a home. The
remarkable thing is we have a choice every day regarding
the attitude we will embrace for that day. We cannot
change our past . . . we cannot change the fact that people
will act in a certain way. We cannot change the inevitable.
The only thing we can do is play on the one string we have,
and that is our attitude . . . I am convinced that life is 10%
what happens to me and 90% how I react to it. And so it is
with you . . . we are in charge of our attitudes.

Charles Swindoll

Footprints

One night a man had a dream. He dreamed he was walking along the beach with the Lord. Across the sky Flashed scenes from his life. For each scene, he noticed two sets of footprints in the sand: one belonging to him and the other to the Lord.

When the last scene of his life flashed before him, he looked back at the footprints in the sand. He noticed that many times along the path of his life there was only one set of footprints. He also noticed that it happened at the very lowest and saddest times in his life.

This really bothered him and he questioned the Lord about it. "Lord, you said that once I decided to follow you, you'd walk with me all the way. But I have noticed that during the most troublesome times of my life, there is only one set of footprints. I don't understand why, when I needed you most, you would leave me."

The Lord replied, "My son, My precious child. I love you and I would never leave you. During your times of trial and suffering, when you see only one set of footprints, it was then that I carried you."

Mary Stevenson

The Serenity Prayer

God, grant me the Serenity
to accept the things I cannot change,
Courage to change the things I can,
and the Wisdom to know the difference.

Living one day at a time,
Enjoying one moment at a time,
accepting hardship as the pathway to peace.
Taking, as He did, this sinful world as it is,
not as I would have it.
Trusting that He will make all things right
if I surrender to His will.
That I may be reasonably happy in this life,
and supremely happy with Him forever in the next.
Amen.

Reinhold Neibuhr

Yesterday, Today, and Tomorrow

There are two days in every week about which we
should not worry, two days which should be kept free
from fear and apprehension.

One of these days is yesterday, with its mistakes and cares,
its faults and blunders, its aches and pains.
Yesterday has passed forever beyond our control.
All the money in the world cannot bring back yesterday.
We cannot undo a single act we performed.
We cannot erase
a single word we said. Yesterday is gone.

The other day we should not worry about is tomorrow,
with its possible adversities, its burdens, its large
promise, and poor performance. Tomorrow is also
beyond our immediate control. Tomorrow's sun will
rise, either in splendor or behind a mask of clouds, but
it will rise. Until it does, we have no stake in tomorrow,
for it is yet to be born.

This leaves only one day – today. Any person can fight the
battles of just one day. It is only when you and I add
the burden of those two awful eternities, yesterday
and tomorrow, that we break down. It is not the
experience of today that drives us mad. It is the
remorse or bitterness of something which happened
yesterday and the dread of what tomorrow may bring.
Let us therefore live but one day at a time.

Anonymous

References

I gratefully acknowledge permission to quote and reprint excerpts from the following:

Cooper, James Fenimore. Drums along the Mohawk. New York: Scribner, 1947. 122-123.

Diamond, Neil. "The Story of My Life." Stonebridge Music, 1986.

Frankl, Viktor E. Man's Search for Meaning. Boston: Beacon, 1967. 65.

Hogan, Ben and Herbert Warren Wind. Five Lessons: The Modern Fundamentals of Golf. Illustrated by Anthony Ravielli. New York: Barnes, 1957. 30.

Holy Bible: King James Version. Nashville: Thomas Nelson, 1984.

Huxley, Aldous. Those Barren Leaves. New York: Harper, 1925. 379-380.

Kittel, Bonnie Pedrotti, Vicki Hoffer, and Rebecca Abts Wright. Biblical Hebrew: A Text and a Workbook. New Haven: Yale UP, 1989. 386.

Sandburg, Carl. "The People, Yes." Complete Poems. New York: Harcourt, 1950. 513.

Schultz, Charles. "Peanuts." Cartoon. United Feature Syndicate. <http://www.snoopy.com/comics/peanuts>.

Smith, Robert H. Dr. Bob and the Good Oldtimers. New York: Alcoholics Anonymous World Services, 1980. 12.

Watterson, Bill. "Calvin and Hobbes." Cartoon. Universal Press Syndicate. <http://www.ucomics.com/calvinandhobbes>.

About the Author

Maurice "Mo" Murray proudly labels himself as "a grateful recovering alcoholic."

He is a retired substance abuse counselor and former clinical director of a large intensive outpatient treatment center in the North East.

He now lives, high up, in a high rise apartment building in the historic district of Charleston South Carolina with his long hair black domestic blind special needs rescue cat, Jackson (as in Stonewall). Jackson has white paw mittens and a white bib [you can see pictures of Jackson on Mo's Amazon Author's Page.]

Mo's apartment overlooks Charleston Harbor and, in the distance, Fort Sumter. Mo, never missing the chance to tell a weak obvious joke, notes that neither have fired any shots lately.

The book "CAR®" is the third of his "How To" Recovery Books.